**ADVANCED
ENGLISH SERIES**

Clauses & Phrases

by C. G. Cleveland

Book cover design by Kathy Kifer

To my brother-in-law
Bob

Published by:
Garlic Press
605 Powers St.
Eugene, OR 97402

ISBN 0-931993-55-5
Order Number GP-055

www.garlicpress.com

Dear Parents, Teachers, and Students:

The Advanced Straight Forward English Series has been designed for parents, teachers, and students. The Advanced Series is designed to measure, teach, review, and master specific English skills. The focus of this book is clauses and phrases.

What makes this Series different?

- Various textbook series have been compared. The Advanced Straight Forward English Series presents the skills crucial to the mastery of clauses and phrases as reflected in major English textbooks.

- Clauses and phrases skills are concisely explained, practiced, and tested.

- Mastery can be measured by comparing the Beginning Assessment Test with the Final Assessment Test.

- The Advanced Series has more content and no distracting or unrelated pictures or words. The skills are straightforward.

How to use this book.

- Give the Beginning Assessment Test to gain a starting measure of a student's knowledge of clauses and phrases.

- Progress through each topic. Work the exercises. Exercises can be done in the book or on a separate sheet of paper. Set a standard to move from one topic to the next. If the standard is not met, go back and refocus on that topic.

- Review practice is periodically given. Use the Review as a simple measurement of skill attainment.

- Give the Final Assessment Test to gain an ending measure of a student's clauses and phrases skills. Compare the skill levels before and after the Final Assessment Test.

Contents

Beginning Assessment Test

Clauses

A.   Is the following a dependent clause (D) or independent clause (I)?

    1.   When I go to the park
    2.   I'm going to the park
    3.   This is a sentence
    4.   Until I finish this job
    5.   Before the ball game starts

B.   Is the following a dependent clause (C) or a phrase (P)?

    1.   After going to lunch
    2.   After I go to lunch
    3.   Since Janelle graduated
    4.   Since finishing high school
    5.   Although saving money is important
    6.   Although I am saving money for a car

C.   Underline the dependent clauses in the following sentences.

    1.   When my dog barks, I jump.
    2.   I returned the sweater that I had borrowed.
    3.   Bob came, as I had asked, to the school.
    4.   After you've watered the garden, wash the windows.
    5.   Come over to my house if you're not busy tonight.

D.   Underline the dependent clause and circle the word it modifies.

    1.   I like the dress that has blue polka dots.
    2.   My face turned red when I tripped and fell.
    3.   We moved twice while Vanessa was still a baby.
    4.   The cat will be mad if you leave it out all night.
    5.   The press, before they could enter, had to show identification.

E.   Indicate if the following underlined clause is used as an Adverb (Adv), Adjective (Adj), or Noun (N).

    1.   <u>Whoever leaves last</u> must lock the door.
    2.   Mom is leaving <u>whether you are ready or not</u>.
    3.   Joan, <u>whose step-mother is my aunt</u>, is my best friend.
    4.   My dog knew <u>that I had a bone behind my back</u>.
    5.   <u>Since I have traveled abroad</u>, I've become more culturally aware.
    6.   I feel sorry for dogs <u>that bark all night</u>.

Verbals and Phrases

A. Identify the underlined verbal in each sentence as a gerund **(Ger)**, a participle **(Part)**, or an infinitive **(Inf)**.

1. I live in a <u>farming</u> community.
2. Sun <u>tanning</u> may be harmful.
3. I plan <u>to win</u> the Irish sweepstakes.
4. I smell <u>burnt</u> rubber.
5. <u>Parenting</u> is not easy.

B. Indicate whether the underlined phrase is gerund **(Ger)**, participial **(Part)**, infinitive **(Inf)**, prepositional **(Prep)**, or appositive **(App)**.

1. <u>Hanging the picture</u> was easy.
2. The book told the story <u>of two stranded mountain climbers</u>.
3. One way to get good grades is <u>reading about many subjects</u>.
4. Parenting, <u>the care of your children</u>, is not easy.
5. I live <u>on a farm</u>.
6. Those ducks <u>climbing out of the pond</u> are cute.
7. <u>Tanning your skin</u> may be harmful.
8. Luis likes <u>to think about his future</u>.
9. My neighbors, <u>angered by the noise</u>, called the police.
10. Martin decided <u>to ski at Big Bear Ski Resort</u>.

C. Identify the underlined phrases as appositive **(App)** or participial **(Part)**.

1. The snake, <u>slithering among the bushes</u>, surprised me.
2. Monica, <u>a fantastic athlete</u>, broke her leg.
3. The man from Africa carried the torch, <u>a distinct honor</u>.
4. My paper, <u>corrected in red pencil</u>, was returned Friday.
5. I tried the impossible, <u>chewing gum and walking at the same time.</u>

D. Identify the underlined parts as appositive phrases **(AP)** or adjective clauses **(AC)**.

1. I attempted the impossible, <u>a death-defying feat</u>.
2. The man from Africa carried the torch, <u>which was a flaming beacon</u>.
3. I haven't been accepted to Harvard, <u>the college of my dreams</u>.
4. Monica, <u>who is a fantastic athlete</u>, broke her leg.
5. *Educating Rita*, an acclaimed movie, was very entertaining.
6. His ankle <u>which was sprained in the fall</u> healed quickly.

Clauses

A **clause** is a group of words that has a subject <u>and</u> a verb. The two types of clauses are independent and dependent.

An **independent** or main clause is a *complete* thought and can stand alone. An independent clause is also known as a sentence.

> *I love dogs.*
> *Mary went to college.*
> *John is my best friend.*

A **dependent** or subordinate clause is an *incomplete* thought and cannot stand alone as a sentence. A dependent clause must accompany an independent clause to make sense. A dependent clause usually begins with a subordinating conjunction or a relative pronoun.

Common **subordinating conjunctions** used in dependent clauses:

after	as soon as	in order that	until
although	as though	since	when/whenever
as	because	so that	where/wherever
as far as	before	than	whether
as if	even though	though	while
as long as	if	unless	

Common **relative pronouns** used in dependent clauses:

that	which	who	whoever
whom	whomever	whose	what

A dependent clause functions as a single part of speech—as an adverb, as an adjective, or as a noun. We, thus, have three types of dependent clauses:

Adverb Clause:	*After I went to the store*, I drove straight home.
Adjective Clause:	I want to buy the dog *that I saw on Sunday.*
Noun Clause:	I've noticed *that Tom can run faster than John.*

Exercise A. In the space provided, indicate if the following clauses are independent **(I)** or dependent **(D)**

1. I love dogs _____
2. If I want a car _____
3. Barbara is a cheerleader _____
4. When I'm sixteen _____
5. If I go away to college _____
6. He would be king _____
7. The eagle soared _____
8. There were three bears _____
9. How the boy looked _____
10. Ever since the puppy licked my face _____

Exercise B. Identify each underlined clause.   Place **I** for an independent clause or **D** for a dependent clause in the space provided.

1. I spotted Jamie under the porch. _____
2. I would have a snack if dinner weren't so soon. _____
3. I like dogs when they are puppies. _____
4. When I grow up, I want to be a rock singer. _____
5. Betty wants to be a singer, too. _____
6. I looked up when I heard the noise on the roof. _____
7. I'll turn eighteen before I graduate. _____
8. When I reached the top of the hill, the weather turned cold. _____
9. Tom isn't here right now. _____
10. Come over when you've finished reading. _____
11. Jason looks older although he's only sixteen. _____
12. When you get home, call me. _____

Exercise C. Underline the dependent clause. (A dependent clause sometimes interrupts an independent clause.)

1. I'll return after I run these errands.
2. I have loved swimming since I was three years old.
3. After I graduate, I want to go to foreign lands.
4. The murderer came to the old mill as Sherlock Holmes had expected.
5. Whatever the circumstances are, Elena will understand.
6. If I hurry through dinner, I'll get an upset stomach.
7. The coat that was by the door is gone.
8. Shops close down around here whenever it snows.
9. She is a person whom I have always admired.
10. When you get here, I'll be ready to go.

Clauses
Adverb

Adverb clauses are dependent clauses used as adverbs. They modify verbs, adjectives, or adverbs. As with all clauses, they contain a subject and a verb.

Adverb clauses always begin with a subordinating conjunction. The subordinating conjunction that introduces the adverb clause establishes a specific relationship to the independent (main) clause. Adverb clauses tell why, when, where, how, under what conditions, or to what extent.

Time:	***After, as, as long as, as soon as, before, until, when, since, whenever,*** and ***while*** *As soon as* I'm settled in Texas, I'll buy a horse.
Place:	***Where*** and ***wherever*** *Wherever* I go, I'm happy to be there.
Condition:	***Even though, if, unless,*** and ***whether*** *Even though* we're poor, we have each other.
Cause:	***As, because,*** and ***since*** I go to school *because* I want a good education.
Purpose:	***So that*** and ***in order that*** I go to school *so that* I can have a better life.
Concession:	***Although*** and ***though*** *Though* Marty is only five, he's expected to do certain chores around the house.
Comparison:	***Than*** Marty has a better vocabulary *than* he had last year.
Manner:	***As, as if,*** and ***as though*** My sister acted *as though* she were a queen.

Adverb clauses modify verbs: My sister **acted** <u>as though she were a queen</u>.

Adverb clauses modify adjectives: <u>Wherever I go</u>, I'm **happy**.

Adverb clauses modify adverbs: I see him **rarely** <u>even though he is my neighbor</u>.

Exercise A. Using the list on the previous page, add a different (if possible) subordinating conjunction before each of the following independent clauses to create dependent clauses.

1. _____ I take the bus every day
2. _____ Jenny is eighteen
3. _____ Donald had a motorcycle
4. _____ June went away to college
5. _____ George has a degree in medicine
6. _____ farmers expect drought this year
7. _____ I am concerned
8. _____ Martha traveled in Japan
9. _____ the bus was late
10. _____ tomorrow is Friday
11. _____ roses are red
12. _____ JFK was President

Exercise B. In the following sentences, underline the dependent adverb clause.

1. <u>If you'll go with us to the hills</u>, I'll prepare a picnic.
2. We had never been apart until she went away to college.
3. Sherman, after he joined the Army, went to Alabama for training.
4. Since the water table dropped last spring, they needed to ration water.
5. Unless you've anything further to add, I suggest we adjourn this meeting.
6. Although Jerry has traveled throughout the U.S., he's never been to Canada.
7. I got to school on time even though the bus was late.
8. While Joe helps kids with reading problems, Jane teaches the hearing impaired.
9. Susan says she'll go wherever Martin goes.
10. Students were idealistic when my mother was in college.

Exercise C. In the following sentences, underline the dependent adverb clause. Circle the verb, adjective, or adverb modified and note which it is at the end of each sentence.

1. He is (confident) <u>before he takes tests</u>. **Adj**
2. Jenny attends college this fall even though she is only sixteen.
3. Sue feels better although she still has a cough.
4. Dad works two jobs so that I can go to college.
5. Singing well didn't come easily until I learned to relax.
6. Since I didn't study, I flunked the math exam.
7. I bought a present for Harold because he fixed my tire last night.
8. I am safe when you hold me.
9. If I had known you were coming, I'd have baked a cake.
10. He eyed my cone longingly while I took my first lick.
11. You've never seen a sunset until you've been to Hawaii.
12. Giselle is happy as long as she gets her way.

> **An adverb clause is quite versatile and can be placed in different parts of the sentence. Notice the position of the comma (if there is one) in each of the following examples.**
>
> *After I went to the store*, I stopped for an ice cream cone.
>
> I stopped for an ice cream cone *after I went to the store.*
>
> I stopped, *after I went to the store*, for an ice cream cone.

Exercise D. Rearrange the sentences in Exercise C so that the dependent adverb clause is in a different part of each sentence. You may have to change the order of the pronoun in some instances for a better sound.

1. <u>Before he takes tests</u>, he is confident.
2. Jenny, <u>even though she is only sixteen</u>, will attend college this fall.
3. _____.
4. _____.
5. _____.
6. _____.
7. _____.
8. _____.
9. _____.
10. _____.
11. _____.
12. _____.

Exercise E. In each of the following sentences, underline the adverb clause, and indicate its relationship to the main clause (i.e., time, place, condition, etc.).

1. I read the Wall Street Journal although it is too sophisticated for me.
    Relationship: _____

2. Ever since I was a child, I've wanted to ride a horse.
    Relationship: _____

3. Jon is going to Stanford University because his dad went there.
    Relationship: _____

4. Unless the weather gets better, we'll all have to stay home.
    Relationship: _____

5.   Time will tell if I will reach my goals.
           Relationship: _____

6.   When you get to the party, call me.
           Relationship: _____

7.   You are smarter than you think.
           Relationship: _____

8.   As far as I can tell, it fits perfectly.
           Relationship: _____

9.   Though I've been to Disneyland often, I never tire of going there.
           Relationship: _____

10.   You are not leaving until I know where you are going.
           Relationship: _____

11.   I must live in France so that my French pronunciation will improve.
           Relationship: _____

12.   You look as if you had seen a ghost.
           Relationship: _____

Clauses
Adjective

Adjective clauses are dependent clauses that are used as adjectives to modify nouns or pronouns.

Adjective clauses often begin with relative pronouns such as: *who, whom, whose, which,* or *that.*

> Jane knows the <u>student</u> **who** *won the scholarship.* (modifies student)
>
> An <u>author</u> **whose** *books I enjoy* is Jack London. (modifies author)
>
> <u>Tom</u>, **whom** *I've known since kindergarden,* was chosen. (modifies Tom)
>
> I like <u>hot dogs</u> **that** *are smothered in mustard.* (modifies hot dogs)
>
> We like <u>stories</u> **which** *have unusual endings.* (modifies stories)

In addition, the relative adverbs *where* and *when* may introduce adjective clauses.

> I remember the <u>store</u> **where** *I bought those shoes.* (modifies store)
>
> Do you remember the <u>time</u> **when** *Lou recited the poem 'Hiawatha'?*
>
> (modifies time)

Adjective clauses almost always follow the noun or pronoun they modify.

Exercise A. Underline the noun or pronoun that is modified by the italicized adjective clause.

1. The police found the dog *which Donald had lost.*
2. Little Jack Horner is the boy *whose Christmas pie was filled with plums.*
3. Come to Rio *where everyone dances in the street.*
4. The place *where the swallows return every year* is Capistrano.
5. These books belong to Betty, *whose pencils I also borrowed.*
6. Maria, *whom I trust implicitly,* went to the bank for me.
7. Dr. Jonas Salk, *who discovered the oral polio vaccine,* continued research all his life.
8. Spring is the season *which I love the most.*
9. The lesson *that I've come to learn* is always tell the truth.
10. I love the ending *when Scarlett says, "Tomorrow is another day."*

15

Exercise B. In the following sentences, underline the dependent adjective clause and circle the noun it modifies. Example: Marcy got the (car) that I wanted.

1.   The doll that I want is porcelain.
2.   A person who speaks Russian will translate.
3.   Could you get those boxes which I left in the corner?
4.   Madrid, which was hot, was a beautiful city.
5.   The scene when Anna trips over Donald's foot is hilarious.
6.   We appreciate the donations, which we sorely need.
7.   My grandmother, whose birthday is next month, will be 98 years old.
8.   The dances that are held on Fridays are sponsored by the Lions' Club.
9.   Some clauses, when they modify a noun or pronoun, are adjective clauses.
10. I put the broom in the corner where the chair is.

Restrictive and Nonrestrictive Clauses

A clause may be essential (necessary) or nonessential (unnecessary) to the meaning of a sentence. Clauses that are essential to a sentence are called **restrictive clauses**. Here are two examples of restrictive adjective clauses:

Students *whose grades are best* may go to the Student Council meeting.

The artifacts *that Ann selected for the exhibit* were from Peru.

In the first example, the meaning would change if the restrictive clause *whose grades are best* was omitted. A nonrestrictive clause would allow all students to go to the Student Council meeting. The intention of this restrictive construction is to limit who goes to the Student Council meeting.

In the second example, the artifacts are not just any artifacts from Peru. They are artifacts that Ann selected specifically for exhibit. Without the restrictive clause, we would not know about Ann, her selection of specific artifacts, nor the exhibit.

Restrictive clauses can be introduced by *that* or *which*.

A clause that is nonessential to the meaning of a sentence is called a **nonrestrictive clause**. Here are two examples of nonrestrictive adjective clauses.

Maria, *who is my friend*, lives across the street.

Our house, *which is grey*, is a historical building.

Both sentences make sense without the adjective clauses. Maria's friendship is incidental to where she lives. The color of the house is incidental to the historical designation of the building.

Why use a nonrestrictive adjective clause, anyway? Nonrestrictive clauses are enhancers. They add color to otherwise bare sentence structures.

Never use *that* to introduce a nonrestrictive clause, and notice that nonrestrictive clauses are set off with commas.

Exercise C. Underline the adjective clause. Indicate if it is restrictive (**R**) or nonrestrictive (**N**).

1.   I like movies that are suspenseful.
2.   Ernest Hemingway is the only American author who always interests me.
3.   There is the dog that won first prize at the kennel show.
4.   She used the hose, which was 50 feet long, to water the garden.
5.   Your grandfather, who lived from 1898 to 1969, worked as an architect.
6.   Shoppers who wish to save money should buy here.
7.   Eugene Skinner, for whom the city of Eugene is named, was an early Oregon pioneer.
8.   Rugby, which is similar to football, is played worldwide.
9.   I decided to attend Mom's *Alma Mater*, which is Radcliff College.
10. The ride to the airport, which usually takes fifteen minutes, took an hour.

Exercise D. Underline the adjective clause. Add commas appropriate to nonrestrictive clauses.

1.   Mary who will be married Saturday is my best friend.
2.   Notice the part that I've set off with commas.
3.   Lonnie who is older than I started college last year.
4.   I'll have the spaghetti that we didn't eat last night.
5.   You are someone whom I don't understand.
6.   The car that needs repair is in the garage.
7.   There was something wrong with the car that we borrowed.
8.   All travelers who arrive late will miss their plane.
9.   Emily who is my neighbor is on vacation.
10. This computer which is in use will be available after 3 o'clock.

Who/Whom and Which/That

The proper use of *who/whom* and *which/that* as relative pronouns is often a chore. While distinctions may be fading in spoken English, a good writer or public speaker must be able to distinguish each. Here are some guidelines.

Who/Whom

Use *who* as the subject of a clause.

> She is the chemist *who made the discovery.*
>> *Who* is the subject of this adjective clause.

Use *whom* as a direct object or as the object of a preposition.

> Mr. Ruiz is the man *whom I met yesterday.*
>> *Whom* is the direct object of met.
> Have you met Mr. Ruiz *from whom I take music lessons?*
>> *Whom* is the object of the preposition *from* (I take lessons *from whom?*).

Who and *whom* can be used to introduce restrictive or non-restrictive clauses. *Who* and *whom* refer to people and sometimes to animals, especially pets.

Exercise E. Fill in the blanks with an appropriate relative pronoun.

1. When you say *that* man, of _____ do you speak?
2. Mitzi, _____ is a star athlete, sprained her ankle.
3. The candidate for _____ I campaigned was untruthful.
4. For _____ does the bell toll?
5. Jack visited Ted _____ graduated last year.
6. So you're the big lunk _____ sent the flowers. Thanks!

Which/That

Which refers to inanimate objects and animals (never people). *Which* is often used to introduce nonrestrictive clauses.

That refers to inanimate objects, animals, and people. *That* is used to introduce restrictive clauses.

Exercise F. Fill in the blanks with an appropriate relative pronoun.

1. The color _____ I like best is red.
2. The puppy_____ I wanted to take home is gone.

3. Bob likes bungee jumping, _____ is a dangerous sport.
4. The Corvette, _____ belongs to Jon, is red.
5. It's time _____ I return home.
6. The food and clothes _____ we collected will go to Bangladesh.

Exercise G. Add an adjective clause to the following independent clauses using the relative pronoun in the parentheses. Remember that each clause must contain a subject and a verb.

1. It's time, _____ , to return home. (*when*)
2. The person _____ is my cousin. (*who*)
3. Madeleine won the gold medal _____. (*that*)
4. Madeleine, _____ , won the gold medal. (*whose*)
5. *Casablanca*, _____ , is a classic. (*which*)
6. Peter, _____ , is always there. (*when*)
7. I'd love to go to Brazil _____ (*where*)
8. This is the country _____ (*that*)
9. I plan to meet some movie stars _____ (*who*)
10. Marie hasn't met Mr. Bernard _____ (*whose*)
11. My grandfather, _____ , was an Olympic skier during the 1930s. (*whom*)
12. In Arizona, _____ , the desert wildflowers are beautiful. (*where*)

Clauses
Noun

Noun clauses are dependent clauses that are used as nouns.

A **noun clause** is used in the same way as a single noun is used. Listed below are some common words used to introduce noun clauses.

how	whatever	which	whomever
if	when	who	whose
that	where	whoever	why
what	whether	whom	

The following examples show some of the ways noun clauses can be used.

Subject:	*Which car we take* isn't important.
Direct Object:	You can believe *whatever you want.*
Predicate Nominative:	The best skis are *whichever ones feel comfortable.*
Object of Preposition:	Mary whines about *whatever task is given her.*

Exercise A. Underline the noun clauses. Write subject **(S)**, direct object **(DO)**, predicate nominative **(PN)**, or object of the preposition **(OP)** in the blank at the end of each sentence.

1.   I don't know what happened. _____
2.   Good grades depend upon how well you study. ___
3.   The deciding factor is whether or not your parents approve. ___
4.   Susan knew that Tom would be there. _____
5.   Whom do you trust is the question. _____
6.   No one knows where Donna lived. _____
7.   Why he's being difficult is anyone's guess. _____
8.   A concern of mine is why you park in handicapped zones. _____
9.   Are you careful about what you say to strangers? _____
10. Mother understood that I forgot to call. _____

Exercise B. Combine one of the dependent clauses with one of the independent clauses and then tell what function it serves: **(S) (DO) (PN) (OP)**.

whatever you want to know	*What Mrs. Jamison said*
Where the boys are	*whoever answers the phone*
When the rivers run dry	*where we are going tonight?*
whomever you designate	*That I can hit a home run*
why the birds fly South in winter	*if you're okay*

1. I will give it to _____. **( )**
2. _____ was hard for me to understand. **( )**
3. To find warmer weather is _____ . **( )**
4. Does Mother know _____. **( )**
5. I want to know _____ . **( )**
6. _____ is where the girls are. **( )**
7. Leave a message with _____ . **( )**
8. _____ is a long shot. **( )**
9. _____ is a long time. **( )**
10. I'll tell you _____ . **( )**

Confusing Noun Clauses with Adjective Clauses

Remember that *who, whom, whose, which,* and *that* may <u>also</u> begin an adjective clause.

The **noun clause** <u>takes the place of</u> the subject or object as in the following examples.

> **Whoever goes to the store** receives a special treat.

>> *Whoever* introduces and is part of the subject of this sentence. The verb *receives* follows the complete subject.

> Max didn't know **who had come to the party.**

>> *Who* introduces and is part of the direct object in this sentence. The verb *didn't know* precedes the direct object.

The **adjective clause** <u>modifies</u> the subject or object.

> The car **which we took to the party** is Warren's.

>> *Which* begins the clause that modifies and follows *car.*

> Everyone ate the pizza **that had just been delivered**.

>> *That* begins the clause that modifies and follows *pizza.*

Exercise C. Identify the following underlined clauses as *adjective* or *noun* in the blanks. Circle the noun modified whenever an adjective clause is found.

1. Whoever needs a ride is welcome to come with us. _____

2. This is the list which has the test scores. _____

3. I'm going to the show that is at four o'clock. _____

4. What I do with my life is my business. _____

5. I guess that I'm the only one who voted this year. _____ _____

6. That I'm not responsible enough to drive is not true. _____

7. You mean the one that is on the top shelf? _____

8. Whatever John says is all right by me. _____

9. Don't take the umbrella that has the red handle. _____

10. How well I do depends on how hard I study. _____ _____

Verbals

Verbals are words which have been formed from verbs but which function as other parts of speech. There are three types of verbals.

Before we are introduced to phrases, we must first learn about verbals because verbals can be expanded to form three of the five major phrase structures.

A **Gerund** is a verb form used as a noun. It always ends in *-ing*.
   <u>Reading</u> is difficult for my brother.

A **Participle** is a verb form used as an adjective. It often ends in *-ing*, but may also end with *-n, -en, -t, -d.*
   The doll, <u>torn</u> and <u>soiled</u>, lay beside the <u>sleeping</u> infant.

An **Infinitive** is a verb form used as a noun, an adjective, or an adverb. It usually begins with *to*.
   They wanted <u>to eat</u>.

Pretest A. Before we explain more about verbals, try these exercises. Identify the underlined verbals as gerund (**Ger**), participle (**Part**), or infinitive (**Inf**).

1.   Bob's on the <u>swimming</u> team. _____
2.   <u>Kneeling</u> is hard on the knees. _____
3.   Jack went <u>to fetch</u> a pail of water. _____
4.   <u>Fallen</u> arches hurt your feet. _____
5.   I want <u>baked</u> beans for dinner. _____
6.   The prince came here <u>to ask</u> for the maiden's hand. _____
7.   I'm tired of <u>reading</u>. _____
8.   It's hard <u>to concentrate</u> when that music is so loud. _____

Pretest B. In the following sentences, tell if the verbal functions as a noun (**N**), an adjective (**Adj**), or an adverb (**Adv**).

1.   <u>To copy</u> this manuscript will take two hours. _____
2.   Get the <u>smelling</u> salts! _____
3.   I ran <u>to find</u> the smelling salts. _____
4.   John enjoys <u>jogging</u>. _____
5.   <u>Gardening</u> takes a lot of patience. _____
6.   I said he was <u>soaking</u> wet! _____

Verbals

Gerund

A **gerund** is a noun which is formed from a verb. It can be used in all the ways a noun can be used. It always ends in *-ing*.

Adding the *-ing* to the verb *swim* makes it possible for us to use the noun *swimming* in the following ways:

> ***Subject*** : <u>Swimming</u> is fun.
> ***Predicate Nominative*** : My favorite activity is <u>swimming</u>.
> ***Direct Object*** : I enjoy <u>swimming</u>.
> ***Object of the Preposition*** : Janice excelled in <u>swimming</u>.
> ***Appositive*** : I have a new favorite pastime, <u>swimming</u>.

Review of the Parts of a Sentence.

The **subject** is a noun (or group of words containing a noun) which tells *who* or *what* the sentence is about. The subject usually precedes the verb.

The **predicate nominative** is a noun (or group of words containing a noun) which renames the subject. The predicate nominative is placed after a linking verb.

The **direct object** is a noun (or group of words containing a noun) that answers the question *what?* or *whom?* It is placed after an action verb.

The **object of the preposition** is a noun within a phrase that begins with a preposition.

The **appositive** is a noun (or group of words containing a noun) that renames another noun. Unlike the predicate nominative, the appositive to a subject usually closely follows the subject.

Gerund Predicate Nominative? or Progressive Verb Form?

Be careful that you do not confuse the gerund form of the predicate nominative with the progressive verb form. Both end in *-ing*. Both follow a form of the verb *to be*. A good guideline to follow is that the predicate nominative always **renames** the subject.

For example:
> Careful <u>timing</u> is <u>important</u> to comedy. (***Timing*** is equal to ***important.***)
> <u>Important</u> to comedy is careful <u>timing</u>. (***Important*** is equal to ***timing.***)

But, in the following sentences, what may appear to be a gerund is really the progressive verb tense which conveys action.

> The cow *is chewing.*
> The bird *has been singing.*
> The girl and boy *were dancing.*

Remember that the predicate nominative can change positions with the subject of the sentence.

The following three exercises will give you practice in determining the difference between a gerund predicate nominative which renames the subject, and the progressive verb tense, which shows action and usually takes an object.

Exercise A. To better understand how the gerund predicate nominative works, (1) underline the subject and the predicate nominative in the following sentences, and (2) switch them as in the example.

> Example: Singing is Susan's greatest love. **Singing** is the subject
> Change to: Susan's greatest love is singing. **love** is the subject

1.   Swimming is a good exercise.
2.   Skiing is my favorite winter sport.
3.   Pouting and whining are some childish tactics.
4.   Writing Haiku is a spring pastime in Japan.
5.   Smoking cigarettes is one sure way to get wrinkles.

Exercise B. Now, place the gerund predicate nominative in the place of the subject.

> Example: Another word for cave exploration is spelunking.
> Change to: Spelunking is another word for cave exploration.

1.   The way to become fit is exercising.
2.   Seeing is believing.
3.   Your great fortune is a blessing.
4.   One of the hardest jobs is farming.
5.   My worst nightmare is failing civics.

Exercise C. Determine if the following underlined *-ing* words are gerunds as predicate nominatives **(PN)** or are the progressive part of the verb *to be* **(PV)**.

1.   Susan was singing in the shower. **(PV)**
2.   We will be seeing you in apple blossom time.
3.   My best summer experience was camping.

4. The shark was <u>circling</u> our boat.
5. The worst part was <u>confessing</u> to Dad.
6. A problem in many towns is <u>drinking</u> and <u>driving</u>.
7. The sky is <u>falling</u>.
8. A child's most important job is <u>attending</u> school.
9. Jody had been <u>sleeping</u> for hours.
10. My chore on Wednesdays is <u>taking</u> out the trash.

The Gerund

The gerund *-ing* verb form acts as subject, predicate nominative, direct object, object of the preposition, or appositive. The following exercises will give you practice in identifying the gerund verbal.

Exercise A. Underline the gerund used as the subject of each sentence. Write the root verb in the infinitive form.

1. <u>Swimming</u> is good exercise. ***to swim***
2. Jogging holds no interest for me.
3. Tap dancing is fun to watch.
4. Shopping is Janet's favorite pastime.
5. Holding all the bags at one time was difficult.
6. Timing is important when you tell jokes.
7. Barbara's teaching while at Johnson High was excellent.
8. Carbon dating is used to determine the age of artifacts.
9. Is eating a good idea before you swim?
10. Sky diving is too dangerous for me!

Exercise B. Underline the gerund as the predicate nominative and circle the subject the gerund describes or renames. (Remember that the predicate nominative and the subject can switch places.)

1. John's (goal) was <u>winning</u>.
2. A dying American art is quilting.
3. Sarah's afternoon ritual was swimming and sunning.
4. Jody's alibi had been sleeping.
5. Part of growing up is learning to compromise.
6. The harshest chore for hands in the old days was washing.
7. A good way to improve your penmanship is rewriting.
8. The best part of cooking is eating.
9. Alexandra's ambition had always been acting.
10. An interesting hobby is stamp collecting.

Exercise C. Underline each gerund used as the direct object.

1.   He teaches <u>writing</u>.
2.   Mary likes ice skating.
3.   The children loved watching the game.
4.   Bobby handled the grocery shopping.
5.   Evelyn learned shooting from her father.
6.   I like wind surfing.
7.   Mother made the turkey stuffing.
8.   Most kids like studying while the radio is on.
9.   The juggler practiced balancing with one hand.
10.   Stop singing so loud!

Exercise D. The following sentences contain the gerund used as the object of the preposition. Underline the gerund and circle the preposition.

1.   This book is (about) <u>hunting</u>.
2.   The girls came for the dancing; the boys came for the food.
3.   The lecture was about drinking and drugs.
4.   Before leaving, please sign the roster.
5.   He started to answer without thinking.
6.   He won the trophy by working hard.
7.   I was leaning toward writing the book myself.
8.   The best of the singing was yet to come.
9.   By telling about my trip, I was able to encourage others to travel.
10.   When it comes to winning, Johnnie is the best.

Exercise E.   Let's see how well you do at spotting gerund verbals as appositives. Think of an appositive as an afterthought that renames or describes the noun it follows. Underline the gerund appositive in each sentence.

1.   The water sport, <u>swimming</u>, is also good exercise.
2.   Dad rarely finds time for his greatest pleasure, fishing.
3.   One art in Japan, drumming, is called Taiko.
4.   This spot will serve our purpose, camping and hiking.
5.   Your destructive behavior, fighting, is more than I can stand.
6.   She had an annoying habit, interrupting.
7.   This task, fencing, is arduous for the rancher.
8.   There's only one word for ocean waves, calming.
9.   This task, collating, is a tedious part of mailing brochures.
10.   The IRS has a challenging job, tax collecting.

Exercise F. Create sentences using the suggested gerunds and the suggested parts: subject (**S**), direct object (**DO**), object of the preposition (**OP**), appositive (**App**), or predicate nominative (**PN**)

1.   shopping **(DO)**

2.   loitering **(App)**

3.   lalling **(S)**

4.   crawling **(PN)**

5.   saving **(OP)**

6.   painting **(DO)**

7.   closing **(S)**

8.   planning **(App)**

9.   dressing **(OP)**

10.   edging **(PN)**

Verbals

Participle

A **participle** is an adjective formed from a verb. It answers the questions: *Which one?* or *What kind?* about the noun or pronoun it modifies. Some endings are: *-ing, -ed, -t, -n,* or *-en.*

In the following examples, each of the underlined words has a **verb** root:

> I studied the clown's <u>painted</u> face for a very long time. *(to paint)*
> Mary was acting like a <u>grown</u> woman. *(to grow)*
> The <u>fallen</u> branches littered the ground. *(to fall)*
> We tried to straighten the <u>bent</u> wire. *(to bend)*
> Ours was the <u>winning</u> team last Saturday. *(to win)*
> Melissa, <u>coughing</u> loudly, finally got my attention. *(to cough)*

Exercise A. In the space provided, write the verb form of the underlined participle.

1. Are you coming to my <u>swimming</u> party? **to swim**
2. By the <u>hurt</u> look on his face, I knew I'd said the wrong thing. _____
3. We finally found the <u>lost</u> gold coins. _____
4. Proper training can develop a good <u>speaking</u> voice. _____
5. The poor, <u>forgotten</u> puppy whined anxiously. _____
6. It was a <u>crying</u> baby that I heard in the woods. _____
7. Nothing smells fresher than newly <u>mown</u> grass. _____
8. <u>Smiling</u> parents watched their children on the playground. _____
9. Betty, <u>standing</u> tall, received the citizenship award. _____
10. <u>Sitting</u> Bull was a famous Indian chief. _____

Exercise B. Underline each participle in the following sentences.

1. Are you part of the <u>swimming</u> team?
2. My pickled beets won first prize at the fair.
3. Have you ever seen Mexican jumping beans?
4. Dried fruit can be a healthy snack.
5. The shorn sheep looked so forlorn.
6. I watched the boxing match with keen interest.
7. Grandmother's hearing aid needed to be repaired.
8. The boys were always looking for buried treasure.
9. Mr. Wilson's grown children surprised him.
10. Tested theories can become facts.

Exercise C. Can you distinguish between a participle and a verb? In the space provided, write verb or participle for the underlined word in each sentence.

1. Not a word was <u>written</u> on his test when the bell rang. _____
   The <u>written</u> word can be a powerful influence. _____
2. That fox <u>poached</u> three chickens from the hen house. _____
   I love <u>poached</u> eggs with bacon and toast. _____
3. Do you like <u>easy-listening</u> music? _____
   Mother said, "I'll <u>listen</u> to you if you <u>listen</u> to me." _____
4. We <u>shredded</u> newspapers to make our pompoms. _____
   The <u>shredded</u> newspapers made nice pompoms. _____
5. The cat <u>dangled</u> from the limb helplessly. _____
   This is not a <u>dangling</u> participle. _____
6. Is there an <u>underlined</u> participle in this sentence? _____
   A word is <u>underlined</u> in this sentence, too. _____
7. <u>Come</u> over to the house tonight. _____
   This <u>coming</u> Saturday, I'm going to the basketball game. _____
8. The <u>stolen</u> papers were in the briefcase. _____
   George <u>stole</u> into the cloak room without being noticed. _____
9. Sports cars often have <u>racing</u> stripes. _____
   The three girls were <u>racing</u> to the next corner. _____
10. I like <u>burnt</u> toast. _____
    The house <u>burned</u> to the ground. _____

Exercise D. In the following sentences, identify the underlined as gerund (**Ger**), participle (**Part**), progressive verb form (**PV**), or verb in the past tense (**V**).

1. <u>Stealing</u> is a crime. _____
2. The kids, <u>laughing</u> and <u>shrieking</u>, loved clowns. _____ _____
3. Rock <u>climbing</u> is quite strenuous. _____
4. I like <u>eating</u> donuts while I am <u>drinking</u> coffee. _____ _____
5. This is my certificate for <u>winning</u> the <u>spelling</u> bee. _____ _____
6. My better subjects are <u>reading</u> and <u>writing</u>. _____ _____
7. As I was <u>driving</u> uphill, the car <u>coughed</u> and <u>sputtered</u> and finally died.

   _____ _____ _____
8. <u>Seeing</u> is <u>believing</u>. _____ _____
9. I'm <u>studying</u> for the exam. _____
10. Those were the best <u>baked</u> beans I've ever eaten. _____
11. It made me mad to see the <u>torn</u> page. _____
12. Mary, <u>feigning</u> innocence, told a lie. _____
13. Joe had been <u>listening</u> intently to the speaker. _____
14. The kids <u>laughed</u> and <u>shrieked</u> at the clowns. _____ _____
15. <u>Waiting</u> impatiently, a <u>frowning</u> passenger checked his watch.

    _____ _____

Verbals
Infinitive

An **infinitive** is a verbal usually beginning with *to*. It is used as a noun, an adjective, or an adverb.

Infinitives have two forms. Most often the word **to** precedes a verb. Occasionally, **to** is omitted. Enclosed in the box are some common infinitive uses.

Noun

        as Subject:

                To swim well takes lots of practice.

                        To swim is the **subject** of this sentence.

        as Direct Object:

                The puppy wants to play.

                        to play is the **direct object** of this sentence.

         as Predicate Nominative:

                The plan is to come early.

                        to come **restates** the subject of this sentence.

        as Appositive:

                My intent, to solve the problem, is not misguided.

                        to solve **restates** the subject of this sentence.

Adjective:

                The best movie to see is playing at The Bijou.

                        The noun subject *movie* is modified by the **adjective** *to see.*

Adverb:

                She strained to hear the speaker.

                        The verb *strained* is modified by the **adverb** *to hear.*

                Mary was happy to see you again.

                        The adjective *happy* is modified by the **adverb** *to see.*

                The fruit is ripe enough to eat.

                        The adverb *enough* is modified by the **adverb** *to eat.*

Review of the Parts of a Sentence.

An adjective is a word that describes a noun or a pronoun by answering the questions *what kind, how many,* or *which one.* It sometimes precedes the noun it modifies; but, when using an infinitive or participle phrase, the adjective most often follows the word it modifies.

An adverb describes a verb, an adjective, or another adverb. It answers the questions *how, when, where,* and *to what extent.* An infinitive adverb often answers the question *why.*

Exercise A. Underline the noun infinitive in each of the following sentences. Tell if it is the subject **(S)**, direct object **(DO)**, or if there is no noun infinitive.

1. To get a job is my summer goal. **(S)**
2. I want to believe in you.
3. I'm trying to listen!
4. I have to ask a question.
5. To cooperate requires communication.
6. Do I have to dance?
7. I'll count to ten.
8. What do you want to be when you grow up?
9. To teach is difficult, but challenging.
10. Jenny asked to leave at noon.

Exercise B. Underline the adjective infinitive, and circle the noun it modifies.

1. The book to read again is *The Adventures of Tom Sawyer* by Mark Twain.
2. The fudge to eat is my mother's.
3. The guy to beat in the swim meet is Jackson.
4. The worst thing to do is to do nothing.
5. Now's the time to shine!
6. The kids have a secret to keep.
7. It's time to begin the program.
8. Grandpa still has enough energy to climb that hill.

Exercise C. Underline the adverb infinitive. Circle the word modified, and indicate if it is an adjective, verb, or adverb.

1. Barbara was happy to return to work. Adj
2. John stayed to find out his grades. _____
3. She listened intently to hear the high notes. _____
4. Is Herbert ready to go? _____
5. Judy studied hard enough to pass chemistry. _____
6. I was sad to see her cry. _____
7. I've been exercising lately to strengthen my biceps. _____
8. It is too dark to walk in the park alone. _____

Exercise D. Underline the infinitives in the following sentences. Tell if the infinitive is a subject **(S)**, direct object **(DO)**, adjective **(Adj)**, or adverb **(Adv)** in the space provided.

1.   I want <u>to be</u> alone. **DO**
2.   Bob hurried to finish his homework. _____
3.   Mother decided to take a ceramics class. _____
4.   To win feels great. _____
5.   Sally plans to attend. _____
6.   She studied hard to earn her diploma. _____
7.   This crossword is hard to do. _____
8.   To complain was a mistake. _____
9.   Children need something to do all the time. _____
10. Mary bought a special dress to wear. _____
11. Are you trying to scare me? _____
12. Your house is difficult to find at night. _____

Phrases

A **phrase** is a group of related words that functions as a single part of speech (i.e., noun, pronoun, verb, adverb, or adjective). A phrase does not have both a subject and a verb.

The five types of phrases are the **gerund phrase**, the **participial phrase**, the **infinitive phrase**, the **prepositional phrase**, and the **appositive phrase**.

The **Gerund Phrase** is used as a noun.
> <u>Picking up litter</u> helps keep our cities clean.

The **Participial Phrase** is used as an adjective.
> The rain, <u>lightly sprinkling</u>, freshened the air.

The **Infinitive Phrase** can serve as a noun, an adjective, or an adverb.
> <u>To know you</u> is <u>to love you</u>. (noun)
> The dress <u>to wear to the prom</u> is the pink one. (adjective)
> I'm leaving <u>to feed the animals</u>. (adverb)

The **Prepositional Phrase** starts with a preposition.
> The Olympiads are going <u>for the gold</u>.

The **Appositive Phrase** renames or explains the adjacent noun or pronoun.
> I thank you, <u>the students of Marysville High</u>, for the invitation.

Three of the five types of phrases are verbal phrases. Unlike verbals which are confined to single words, phrases contain several words but include a verbal within the phrase.

Exercise A. Indicate if the underlined words are a **single** verbal or part of a verbal **phrase**. State **single** or **phrase** in the spaces provided.

1. Soccer is <u>challenging</u>. _____
2. <u>Listening</u> intently to the tape, I learned to speak Japanese. _____
3. Tennis, a <u>challenging</u> sport, is also fun. _____
4. I said, "It's no fair <u>peeking</u>!" _____
5. Okay, the dinner is <u>done</u>. _____
6. I've come to a <u>startling</u> conclusion. _____

7. At the check-out, Dad forgot <u>to pay</u>. _____

8. <u>Watching</u> is an important part of <u>learning</u>. _____ _____

9. The news, <u>reported</u> from Somalia, had a <u>chilling</u> impact upon me. _____ _____

10. <u>Coming</u> to theaters everywhere, this movie is a real thriller. _____

Exercise B. Decide if the underlined phrases in the following sentences are verbal phrases (gerund, participle, or infinitive), prepositional phrases, or appositive phrases.

1. <u>Cornered by the cat</u>, the rat made a dash <u>up the wall</u>.
2. Ruth Ann, <u>swinging her legs as she rocked</u>, spoke <u>with a lisp</u>.
3. The horse, <u>a tired, old swayback</u>, managed <u>to plod along</u>.
4. The storm's center was near Georgia, <u>the Peach State</u>.
5. I've made progress <u>in publishing Grandpa's memoirs</u>.
6. Two roads diverged <u>in a wood</u>.
7. The cherry blossoms <u>falling upon the sidewalk</u> look <u>like new-fallen snow</u>.
8. <u>To point out your mistakes for you</u> would be unkind.
9. Let's go <u>to the root of the problem</u>, <u>your attitude</u>.
10. Follow the map <u>drawn by Greg</u> and you'll have no trouble.

Phrases

Gerund

The **gerund phrase** is a group of words which includes the gerund verbal and is used as a noun substitute. The gerund always ends in *-ing*.

A gerund can be used in all the ways a noun can be used.

> **Subject:**
>> Swimming alone is dangerous.
>>> The gerund Swimming and the adverb *alone* consitiute the gerund phrase and act as the subject of this sentence.
>
> **Direct Object:**
>> I love swimming in the ocean.
>>> Swimming plus the prepositional phrase *in the ocean* act as the direct object of this sentence.
>
> **Object of the Preposition:**
>> I strengthened my muscles by swimming in the ocean.
>>> Swimming plus the prepositional phrase *in the ocean* act as the object of the preposition *by.*
>
> **Predicate Nominative:**
>> An enjoyable pastime is swimming in the ocean.
>>> The gerund swimming plus the prepositional phrase *in the ocean* rename the subject *pastime.*
>
> **Appositive:**
>> This water sport, competition swimming, is one of the most enjoyable to watch.
>>> Competition swimming explains and renames *water sport.*

Exercise A. Underline the gerund phrase in the following sentences. Indicate if the phrase is used as subject (**S**) or direct object (**DO**) in each sentence.

1.   Going along with the crowd isn't always the smart thing to do. **(S)**
2.   Honing his tennis skill took up all his spare time.
3.   This exercise requires lying on your back.

4. Identifying the gerund is sometimes difficult.
5. I like swimming in our pool.
6. Falling off a bicycle is not easy!
7. Courage means standing up for yourself.
8. Substituting sweetener for sugar makes the cake less caloric.
9. The next section of the test requires filling in the blanks.
10. Standing up for yourself takes a lot of courage.

Exercise B. Fill in the following blanks with a gerund to complete the phrase. Indicate if it is the subject (**S**), direct object (**DO**), object of the preposition (**OP**), appositive (**App**), or predicate nominative (**PN**) at the end of each sentence.

1. The most difficulty John had last season was <u>pitching</u> *a no hitter.* **(PN)**
2. _____ *you to drive* has made me nervous.
3. Bobby started _____ *baseball cards* when he was six years old.
4. I like _____ *people in need.*
5. My job, _____ *at the factory,* ended yesterday.
6. Say grace *before* _____ .
7. The responsibility of every adult should be _____ *their children from harm.*
8. *The* _____ *for the criminals* is next Tuesday.
9. *After* _____ *alcohol,* don't drive!
10. _____ *for the exam* takes a lot of time.
11. The city's plan is _____ *that old building.*
12. _____ *to tie shoelaces* is difficult for a two-year-old.

Exercise C. Make sentences using the following gerund phrases in the suggested manner.

1. walking in the park *(subject)*
2. attending day care *(predicate nominative)*
3. spending too much money *(object of the preposition)*
4. living as a hermit *(direct object)*
5. working at the dime store *(appositive)*
6. feeding the animals *(direct object)*
7. choosing the right person for the job *(subject)*
8. choosing the right person for the job *(appositive)*
9. complete understanding *(direct object)*
10. testing each other *(predicate nominative)*

Exercise D. In the following sentences, distinguish between a progressive verb **(PV)** and the gerund predicate nominative **(PN)**. If a predicate nominative, finish underlining the phrase.

1. The art of bonsai is <u>pruning trees to remain small</u>. **(PN)**.
2. It is <u>raining</u> cats and dogs outside.
3. Martin has been <u>learning</u> the piano for seven years.
4. A relaxing pastime for me is <u>fishing</u> at the old river pond.
5. I will be <u>sailing</u> at Fern Ridge Lake next weekend.
6. The glider was <u>soaring</u> over the empty field.
7. The best part of the day is <u>relaxing</u> in the tub.
8. His first gig was <u>playing</u> at the Hungry I in San Francisco in the 1950s.
9. My baby brother will be <u>walking</u> soon.
10. Brahms' music is <u>soothing</u> to the ear.

Exercise E. Identify the underlined gerund phrases as subject **(S)**, predicate nominative **(PN)**, direct object **(DO)**, object of the preposition **(OP)**, or appositive **(App)**.

1. Sandra is very fast at <u>counting money</u>.
2. *Sawing logs*, <u>sleeping soundly</u>, is a slang term.
3. The most difficult event at the track meet was <u>pole vaulting</u>.
4. <u>Proclaiming the defendent guilty</u> was the jury's verdict.
5. I like <u>eating peanut butter and jelly sandwiches</u>.
6. <u>Dancing in the garden</u> gave Wanda great pleasure.
7. Veterans Day is a time for <u>remembering the people who defend our country</u>.
8. Grudges, <u>the harboring of bad feelings towards others</u>, are not healthy.
9. Marsha gave <u>the blessing at dinner</u>.
10. An important job at the grocery store was <u>restocking the shelves</u>.

Exercise F. Change the following verbs into gerunds, and create sentences containing gerund phrases. You must have five (5) sentences for each verb. Study the examples.

<u>Example:</u>   verb: to collect   **change to** gerund verbal: collecting

Subject: <u>Collecting stamps</u> is my hobby.
Predicate Nominative: My hobby is <u>collecting stamps</u>.
Direct Object: My brother likes <u>collecting old comic books</u>.
Object of the Preposition: John was rewarded for <u>collecting the most signatures</u>.
Appositive: My hobby, <u>collecting Japanese dolls</u>, began ten years ago.

1.   to join
2.   to learn
3.   to bicycle
4.   to wash
5.   to play

Phrases

Participle

The **participial phrase** is a group of related words used as an adjective. The participle often ends in *-ed, -ing, -n, -en, -t,* or *-d.*

In the examples below, notice that a participial phrase can be at the beginning, middle, or end of a sentence.

Participle with a prepositional phrase:
The pool <u>built in our yard</u> is 30 feet long.
The participle *built* together with the prepositional phrase "in our yard" modifies the noun *pool.*

Participle with an adverb:
<u>Landing roughly</u>, the plane finally glided to a stop.
The participle *landing* together with the adverb "roughly" modifies the noun *plane.*

Participle with a noun complement:
The girl <u>playing the piano</u> is my friend.
The participle *playing* together with its noun complement "piano" modifies the noun *girl.*

Exercise A. Underline the participial phrases and circle the participles. (Remember that the participle is a verbal.)

1. That noise (coming) from the engine of my car really worries me.
2. Ruined by the rain, the dress could never be worn again.
3. Now roasted to a golden brown, the turkey was ready to eat.
4. These words coming from your father require your attention.
5. Rock music records collected by my father are now classics.
6. My brother, hunting in the backwoods at thirteen, found a baby fox.
7. Feeling good, the three boys pitched in to buy ice cream cones.
8. The demented scientist creeping toward the heroine was played by Lon Chaney.
9. Extra caution must be taken by those students driving their cars.
10. Stealth bombs launched at night are very scary.

Exercise B. In the following sentences, circle the main word being modified by the underlined participial phrases.

1.   That (noise) coming from the engine of my car really worries me.
2.   Ruined by the rain, the dress could never be worn again.
3.   That tiny kitten sitting alone in the corner is the one I want.
4.   Clearly chirping away, the canary hadn't a care in the world.
5.   Rock music collected by my father is now a classic.
6.   My brother, hunting in the backwoods at thirteen, found a baby fox.
7.   Feeling good, the three boys pitched in to buy ice cream cones.
8.   The demented scientist creeping toward the heroine was Lon Chaney.
9.   Extra caution must be taken by those students driving their cars.
10.   Stealth bombs launched at night are very scary.

Exercise C. Underline the participial phrase which modifies the circled noun. In the blanks provided, tell if the phrase contains an **adverb**, a **preposition**, a **noun complement**, or is a **single** participle.

1.   What's that (noise) coming from the cemetery? _____
2.   Listening acutely, (I) heard the high pitched sound. _____
3.   (Joan) mocking her brother, pulled a long face. _____
4.   Carrying his daughter, (Mr. Carter) seemed a happy man. _____
5.   The (puppy) was so frisky, running across the back lawn. _____
6.   (Dad) living in Arkansas as a youth, hunted in the Ozarks. _____
7.   The old, starved (buzzard) was hunched on the fence. _____
8.   (Muskrats) playing in the stream look harmless. _____
9.   The artist produced a small (elephant,) exquisitely carved. _____
10.   Launched nightly, the stealth (bombers) could barely be heard. _____

Exercise D. In the following sentences, underline the phrase and identify it as gerund, participle, or progressive verb tense.

1.   He heard the screeching of the brakes.
2.   Mark, shaking violently, was in shock.
3.   Wearing only a nightshirt, he relived the horrible scene for us.
4.   I had been sleeping soundly.
5.   The alarm of dogs, the sharp barking, had awakened me.
6.   The tire marks streaked across the road made me shudder.
7.   Mark, tired of telling the story, wanted to forget the incident.
8.   His greatest wish was falling asleep quickly.
9.   The dogs were sleeping peacefully now.
10.   Holding his hand tightly, I walked Mark to his room.

Punctuating Phrases

Punctuation for phrases, participial or otherwise, is the same as the punctuation we use for restrictive and nonrestrictive clauses. Essential (restrictive) elements do not require punctuation. Nonessential (nonrestrictive) elements require punctuation. In order to determine the necessity of commas, decide if the sentence needs the phrase for complete understanding.

Essential: The clothes <u>flapping in the breeze</u> reminded me of my childhood. (We need to know *which* clothes reminded me of my childhood.)

Nonessential: Karen, <u>acting alone</u>, sneaked into the theater. (We already know *who* sneaked into the theater.)

There is one variation: phrases which <u>begin</u> a sentence are always followed by a comma. This comma, however, is not a signal of nonrestriction. The same two sentences from above <u>introduced</u> by the same two phrases need a comma.

<u>Flapping in the breeze</u>, the clothes reminded me of my childhood.
<u>Acting alone</u>, Karen sneaked into the theater.

Exercise E. Punctuate the participial phrases in the following sentences correctly, when necessary.

1. *Assuming a relaxed attitude* Bobby walked onto the stage.
2. Jill loved wool skirts and sweaters *woven in Ireland.*
3. Marty *completely absorbed in the book* hadn't noticed me.
4. The cookies *baked by Joan's mother* are chocolate chip.
5. Corinne *afraid of getting wet* waited inside the building.
6. She forgot her homework *lying on the kitchen table.*
7. *Having fought the good fight* the football team headed for the showers.
8. The scream *coming from the building* alarmed me.
9. Tell those dogs *barking in the backyard* to stop.
10. *Assured of winning the gold* Maria began to relax a little.

Misplaced Modifiers

Phrases and clauses can be used as modifiers. Participial phrases, as well as other phrases, should be placed as close to the word they modify as possible. When placed too far from the word they modify, they become misplaced modifiers. By placing the participial phrase closer to the noun it modifies, a writer or speaker assures clarity.

Example 1. We enjoyed the autumn leaves <u>walking along the path</u>.

Does the phrase modify <u>leaves</u>? Were the leaves walking along the path? A better construction would be to place the participial phrase closer to the pronoun, *we* , which it modifies.

<u>Walking along the path</u>, we enjoyed the autumn leaves. Or,
Tim and I, <u>walking along the path</u>, enjoyed the autumn leaves.

Example 2. The rabbit was found by Elena <u>hiding behind the door</u>.

What does the phrase modify? Who was hiding behind the door, the rabbit or Elena? A better construction would be to place the phrase closer to the noun, *rabbit* , which it modifies.

Elena found the rabbit <u>hiding behind the door</u>.

Exercise F. Correct the following misplaced modifers. Punctuate with commas where needed.

1.   That noise really worries me coming from my engine.
2.   That puppy is the one I want sitting alone in the corner.
3.   My brother found a baby fox hunting in the woods.
4.   My sister is in another world playing her violin.
5.   The race car ran into the embankment screeching out of control.
6.   Caught in a trap, my brother found a raccoon.
7.   I had a cold all week in the nose.
8.   Hanging on a hook in the closet, he discovered his windbreaker.
9.   A prospector found uranium using his Geiger counter.
10.   Ruined by the rain, I hid the dress so Mother wouldn't see.

Dangling Participles

When participial phrases do not modify anything, they are called dangling participles.

> Walking over the hill, the valley lay in all its splendor.
> > What does the phrase modify? Who or what is "walking over the hill"?
> A better sentence is:

> Walking over the hill, we saw the valley in all its splendor.

The phrase now modifies the subject, *we*. Other changes to the basic sentence smooth out the rough edges. Here's another example:

> Dressing for work, it started to rain. Who or what is "dressing for work"?
> A better sentence is:
> > Dressing for work, I noticed it was starting to rain.

Exercise G. Correct these dangling participles to show *who* or *what* is being modified. Don't be afraid to change or add words to the basic sentence. Try hard not to create dependent clauses out of the participial phrases.

1. Awakened suddenly, the night seemed oddly silent.
2. Listening at the door, there was an argument.
3. Wearing a new designer suit, the executive's office was entered confidently.
4. The theater was impressive, approaching the front entrance.
5. Searching under the bed, the kitten peered out at me.
6. Several deer were seen driving through the Redwood Forest.
7. Focusing the microscope, bacteria could be seen.
8. Turning the wheel sharply, it went out of control and crashed into the railing.
9. I had to eat standing up.
10. Sleeping in the rain, a cold was developed.

Phrases

Infinitive

An **infinitive phrase** is a group of related words used as a noun, an adjective, or an adverb. The word *to* introduces most infinitive phrases.

An infinitive phrase can be used in any way that a noun can be used: as a subject, as a predicate noun, or as a direct object.

Noun phrase

as subject:

To reach this conclusion took a lot of study.
To reach this conclusion is the subject.

as direct object:

I need to reach the top shelf.
To reach the top shelf is the direct object of the verb *need.*

as predicate nominative:

Her goal is to reach 30 push-ups.
To reach 30 push-ups renames the subject *goal.*

An infinitive phrase that modifies a noun or pronoun is used as an adjective.

Adjective phrase:

Elena is the person to see about stamp collecting.
To see about stamp collecting modifies the noun *person.*

An infinitive phrase that modifies a verb, adjective or adverb is used as an adverb, and answers the question *why.*

Adverb phrase:

Mary tried to find out the answer to the questions.
To find out the answer to the questions modifies the verb *tried.*

Marty was sad to leave his friends.
To leave his friends modifies the adjective *sad.*

Lavonne pulled hard to ring the bell.
To ring the bell modifies the adverb *hard.*

Exercise A. Underline the infinitive phrase used as a noun. Circle each infinitive. Indicate if the phrase represents the subject **(S)**, direct object **(DO)**, or predicate nominative **(PN)** in the sentence.

1. The toughest part of the test will be (to answer) the essay questions.**(PN)**
2. I want to drive to the show.
3. To know your own mind shows you're growing up.
4. Mary refused to walk to school today.
5. I'm planning to attend the conference.
6. To bend the rules for you would indicate that I'm wishy-washy.
7. The hardest lesson you'll ever learn is to show humility.
8. To set a good example for your brother is a heavy burden.
9. I don't want to sit here alone.
10. Your job before you leave the house is to make your bed.

Exercise B. Underline the infinitive phrase used as an adjective. Circle the word being modified.

1. Judy's the (one) to watch in the swimming competition.
2. We get pork chops to eat tonight.
3. Judy has the right to speak out on these issues.
4. I had a chance to get a bargain.
5. The person to follow out the door is Judy.
6. We were the first to buy tickets to the concert.
7. The firemen were the only people to notice the gathering crowd.
8. Your trip to see the famous Wellington Gardens sounds fascinating.
9. The first person to finish in under two minutes will set a record.
10. I know it is a heavy burden to set a good example for your brother.

Exercise C. Underline the infinitive phrase used as an adverb. Circle the word modified and indicate if it is a verb **(V)**, an adjective **(Adj)**, or an adverb **(Adv)**.

1. I'm (sorry) to hear the news.   **Adj**
2. Bill really stretched to catch the fly ball.
3. We were too tired to continue the search.
4. Mary tiptoed to keep from being heard.
5. I was pleased to appear on television.
6. She labored to discover the cause of the disease.
7. Graham had studied enough to pass his tests.
8. Stan shopped to make himself happy.
9. Emily seemed content to read for long hours.
10. We all ran to see the fire.

Exercise D. Identify each underlined infinitive phrase as **(S)**, **(DO)**, **(PN)**, **(Adj)**, or **(Adv)**.

1.   She was supposed <u>to join the Peace Corps</u>.**(Adv)**
2.   Do you want pork chops <u>to eat for dinner</u>?
3.   <u>To get into trouble</u> took very little effort.
4.   Jane struggled <u>to eat carrots for good eyesight</u>.
5.   My wish is <u>to be alone right now</u>.
6.   His intent <u>to wear the baseball cap to the prom</u> was inappropriate.
7.   Martha was the only woman <u>to say she believed the story</u>.
8.   I expect <u>to get to the bottom of this</u>.
9.   Good soldiers are the ones <u>to be brave in a conflict like this</u>.
10.   <u>To wait and see</u> is not my style.
11.   I have decided <u>to get off this merry-go-round</u>!
12.   Diversity is important <u>to maintain this great nation</u>.

Exercise E. Make a sentence from each infinitive phrase using the words in parentheses as guides. Study the examples.

<u>Examples</u>:   -to win the sweepstakes **(PN)**
          The object is to win the sweepstakes.

          -to find her real mother. **(S)**
          To find her real mother has taken her 5 years.

          -to get a newspaper **(Adv)**
          Paul rushed to get a newspaper at the corner stand.

          -to pursue a college degree. **(Adj)**
          Joan was the first in her family to pursue a college degree.

          -to go to Princeton **(DO)**
          Sarah intends to go to Princeton.

1.   to drive a car **(S)**
2.   to select the college **(Adv)**
3.   to let the bird go free **(DO)**
4.   to solve the problem **(Adj)**
5.   to collect insurance **(PN)**
6.   to benefit from the experience **(Adv)**
7.   to choose a puppy **(S)**
8.   to get to the game **(Adj)**
9.   to grow up **(Adv)**
10.   to get a good job **(PN)**

Phrases

Prepositional

A **prepositional phrase** is a group of related words that begins with a preposition and ends with a noun or a pronoun called the *object of the preposition.* A prepositional phrase is used as an adjective or an adverb, generally indicating position or direction.

A prepositional phrase functions as an **adjective** when it describes a noun or pronoun.   It usually follows the noun or pronoun that it modifies.

> A **story** in the newspaper described her life.
> We enjoyed the **museums** of art and natural history.
> The flower shop sold **books** about different **kinds** of flowers.

A prepositional phrase that functions as an **adverb** describes a verb, adjective, or adverb. It usually follows the verb or adjective it describes.

> The story **begins** in Canada. (modifies the verb *begins*)
> The trees were **green** at the top. (modifies the adjective *green*)
> Birds often chirp **early** in the morning. (modifies the adverb *early*)

Exercise A. Make a phrase from the following prepositions. Do <u>not</u> make a complete sentence at this time. Study the following examples.

> -*to* the store.
> -*about* six o'clock?
> -*in* a hurry.
> -*for* Sandy's mother.
> -*near* the center *of* town.

1.   at
2.   beneath
3.   from
4.   below
5.   past

6. next to
7. on
8. behind
9. toward
10. about

Exercise B.   Using the following prepositions, create sentences with prepositional phrases acting as adjectives.   Study the following examples.

Mom bought the gift **for** Sandy's mother.
Stories **about** the Old West fascinate me.

1. near
2. upon
3. to
4. beneath
5. in
6. from
7. outside
8. toward
9. with
10. over

Exercise C.   Using the following prepositions, create sentences with prepositional phrases acting as adverbs.   Study the following examples.

I'm going **to** the grocery store.
We live **near** the center of town.

1. across
2. in
3. about
4. by
5. between
6. for
7. outside
8. under
9. during
10. beside

Exercise D. Indicate which of the underlined phrases are adjectives **(Adj)** (modifying nouns or pronouns) and which are adverbs **(Adv)** (modifying verbs, adjectives, or other adverbs). Circle the word being modified. Study the examples below. (Caution: Modifiers of verbals are always adverbs.)

Snakes slither across the grass. *(adv. modifies verb "slither")*
We will begin the meeting of the Elk's Club. *(adj. modifies noun "meeting")*

1. The senator <u>from Tennessee</u> spoke.
2. The senator from Tennessee spoke <u>for 45 minutes</u>.
3. We stayed <u>on her houseboat</u>.
4. We stayed on the houseboat <u>on the Sacramento River</u>.
5. The drive <u>to the general store</u> was fun.
6. Driving <u>in the Model A</u> to the general store was fun.
7. Driving once again to the general store <u>near Wedge Creek</u> was fun.
8. The eagle <u>above me</u> soared.
9. Above me, the soaring eagle was searching <u>for food</u>.
10. The eagle soared effortlessly <u>above me</u>.

Exercise E. Circle each preposition and underline its phrase. Indicate whether the phrase serves as an adjective **(Adj)** or as an adverb **(Adv)**. (Caution: Some sentences have more than one prepositional phrase and some have none**.**)

1. We went to the party together. **Adv**
2. The trip to Yosemite National Park was the highlight of my senior year.
3. Bobby will drive me to your house before noon.
4. Mary hopes to sing with the Metropolitan Opera Company someday.
5. Mr. Graham told me to stand between the goal posts.
6. Dancing in the moonlight is very romantic.
7. My family has known Mr. and Mrs. Downs for many years.
8. I'll be ready in a minute!
9. I knew in a moment it must be St. Nick.
10. Have you seen my jacket with the yellow buttons?
11. I want to visit Paris during the springtime.
12. The sand is cool under the boardwalk.
13. The puppy upon the porch is mine.
14. Jerry is to begin his dive soon.
15. I'm just mad about Saffron.

Phrases

Appositive

An **appositive phrase** is a group of words acting as a noun that renames or explains an adjacent noun or pronoun in the sentence. It is often, but not always, enclosed within commas.

CAUTION: Be sure not to confuse your appositive phrase with an adjective clause.

Adjective Clause: The adjective clause contains both a verb and an introductory relative pronoun.

> Mary, <u>who is a real sleepy head</u>, can sleep through anything.

Appositive Phrase: The appositive phrase doesn't contain a verb.

> Mary, <u>a real sleepy head in the morning</u>, can stay up all night studying.

NOTE: "A real sleepy head in the morning" contains the prepositional phrase <u>in the morning</u>, but the whole phrase is an appositive (or explanation) about "Mary."

Study these examples: Each underlined appositive identifies the noun it renames.

- I'm reading the story <u>*Gone With the Wind*</u>. (identifies the story)
- Jane Hall, <u>the best cellist in our school,</u> will study at Juliard. (renames Jane Hall)
- This class, <u>History of French Cooking</u>, begins at 11 o'clock. (identifies the class)
- My trip last summer, <u>a lengthy trek up the Andean Alps</u>, was the highlight of my life. (renames the trip)

Exercise A. Underline each appositive phrase and circle the noun or pronoun renamed.

1. (Spring,) <u>the season of renewal,</u> is the best time to view cherry blossoms.
2. I often go to my aunt's guesthouse, the cottage on Bridge Street, after school.
3. My dad plays the clarinet, his favorite instrument.

4. I used to play *Old Maid*, an old-fashioned card game, as a child.
5. My golf ball, a nubby green comet, hit a tree before dropping into the hole.
6. Bonsai, the Japanese art of growing miniature trees, instills awe within me.
7. Joe's Master's thesis, a paper chronicling 14th Century Russia, was brilliant.
8. I was up at 1 a.m., the ghostly hour of the night.
9. Zane Grey's books, vivid descriptions of the Southwest, are very exciting.
10. *The Grapes of Wrath*, a book about the Dust-Bowl Era, was made into a movie.

Exercise B. Indicate which of the underlined parts are appositive phrases (**AP**) and which are adjective clauses (**AC**).

1. I loved your speech, *"Coming of Age in the 90s."*
2. I loved your speech that discussed coming of age in the 90s.
3. The kitten, a little ball of fluff, slept in the shoe box.
4. The kitten, which was a little ball of fluff, slept in the shoe box
5. My sister was born December 7, 1941, the day Pearl Harbor was bombed.
6. My sister, who was born at Pearl Harbor, is a pilot.
7. You, the school representative, should know better!
8. You, who are the school representative, should know better.
9. The man who wore the plaid scarf had it wrapped around his neck.
10. The scarf, a plaid one, was wrapped around his neck.

Exercise C. Insert one of the following phrases in an appropriate slot in the following sentences to form an appositive phrase.

a. a nervous giggle
b. the act of making life easier to understand
c. the symbol for *and*
d. the Queen and the Double
e. the Salk vaccine
f. best in show
g. a much needed respite
h. a popular children's book
i. that special stew Mother made last night
j. *Mondo Kane*

1. The oral medicine for polio, _____ , was perfected in the 1950s.
2. The foreign film _____ was quite shocking when I was a teenager.
3. The prize, _____ , went to the Australian Shepherd.
4. John ate the last of the ragout, _____ .
5. Do you know when to use the ampersand, _____ ?
6. Simplifying problems, _____ , is a knack.
7. We took a break, _____ .
8. Maureen's laugh, _____ , showed she was uncomfortble.
9. We offer two sizes, _____ .
10. *The Cat in the Hat*, _____ , is available at the public library.

Exercise D. Underline and label the appositive phrases **(AP)** and those that are participle phrases **(PP)**. Remember that participial phrases use verbals as adjectives.

Study these examples.

- Sarah, <u>gazing out over the fields</u>, stood in the doorway of the cabin. **(PP)**
- Sarah, <u>the woman in the doorway of her cabin,</u> gazed out over the fields. **(AP)**

1.   I achieved my goal, running the one-minute mile, last Friday.
2.   The iron, searing hot metal, was ready to be used for branding the calves.
3.   The heroine, gagged and bound with tape, was left in front of the train.
4.   The concerned group, farmers from Iowa and Kansas, came to meet with the President of the United States.
5.   Your ideas concerning the new health care plan will be reviewed tomorrow.
6.   "The Happening," my party tomorrow night, will be an exciting event.

Exercise E. Change the following participle phrases in some way to become appositive phrases.

1.   The cigar, casting an acrid smell up three floors, belonged to Mr. Chan.
2.   Gary Cooper, acting the tall and handsome stranger, was a popular screen idol.
3.   The puppy, curled into a small white ball, was a Samoyed.
4.   Bells, tinkling as the wind blew, hung from the porch.
5.   Stopped at the red light, the hot-rodder revved his engine impatiently.

Final Assessment Test

Clauses

A. Underline the clauses and determine which are adverb, adjective, or noun.

1. Leslie finally knows why good grades are important to his future. _____

2. Whichever team I choose is sure to win. _____
3. Africa, which is a huge country, has many different tribes. _____
4. I'll be stationed in Somalia, where the Peace Corps is needed so much. _____

5. He knew where to find the body. _____
6. The party starts when you arrive. _____
7. Is this the way which is best? _____
8. Call me from wherever you are. _____
9. Watson came after Sherlock had called. _____
10. He came to make new friends who enjoyed playing chess. _____

B. Underline the noun clause in each sentence, and determine if it serves as the subject, direct object, predicate nominative, or object of preposition.

1. We'll take whichever route is quicker. _____
2. Whoever makes a ruckus goes directly home. _____
3. I'm not sure about where I'll be staying in France. _____
4. Five dollars is how much money you'll need. _____
5. Martin is taking whoever says "yes" first to the prom. _____

C. Underline the adverb clause in each sentence, and circle the word it modifies. Indicate in the space provided if the circled word is a verb, an adjective, or an adverb.

1. Jennie jumped after I yelled "boo!" _____
2. David was cautious while he drove his dad's car. _____
3. This pie tastes good even though I don't usually eat rhubarb. _____
4. I feel better than I did a week ago. _____
5. Fido eyed the mailman warily until he was out of sight. _____
6. We can ride together unless you'd prefer to drive your own car. _____

D.   Underline the clauses in the following sentences, and indicate if they are adjective clauses or noun clauses.

1.   The duckling that had been ugly became a beautiful swan. _____
2.   The butterfly exemplifies that which is elusive in life. _____
3.   Dorothy asked about which road leads to the Emerald City. _____
4.   Who had asked the question in the first place had been long forgotten. _____
5.   That singer who sang the aria also likes to sing jazz. _____

Verbals and Phrases

A.   Underline each verbal. Indicate if it is a gerund, a participle, or an infinitive.

1.   My father has a sprained back.
2.   The worst part of having a cold is the coughing.
3.   Listening is part of learning.
4.   I was taught to control my anger in public.
5.   Have you seen the soldering iron?
6.   Placing the cool towel on my brow helped to soothe my fever.
7.   The solemn-faced boy stood bravely.
8.   Rolfing is a technique for improving one's posture.
9.   "Sufferin' succotash!" cried Sylvester, the cat.
10.   It is time to change for dinner.

B.   Underline the phrases and indicate whether they are gerund, participle, infinitive, prepositional, or appositive. There may be more than one phrase.

1.   Pressing our ears against the ground, we could hear the train coming.
2.   The dog, scratching his ear, groaned with ecstasy.
3.   You can be sure to count on me.
4.   Are you going to the opera tomorrow night?
5.   It's only a game, a silly prank, for your benefit.
6.   Why, I do believe that girl is seething with envy!
7.   The Munchkins, pointing the way to Oz, wore bright colors that day.
8.   To simplify matters even further, I suggest that we all go together.
9.   I've seen *Wizard of Oz*, a whimsical musical, seventeen times.
10.   The lawyer specializing in accident claims has an office in this building.

C.   Punctuate the following with commas, where necessary.

1.   He doesn't know which way is up.
2.   Sometimes when I'm lonely I think of you.
3.   If you are in the neighborhood drop by.
4.   The books that have gold lettering on the cover are mine.
5.   Stop whatever you are doing.

D.   If the sentence contains a misplaced modifying phrase, make corrections.

    1.   The books were given away faded from age.
    2.   I'll drop by when it's convenient for you to pick up my sister.
    3.   He ran with the glove held high after the ball.
    4.   Donna still manages to keep her home immaculate as a working mother.
    5.   The greasy spoon is on the counter which you forgot to wash.

E.   If the sentence contains a dangling participial phrase, make corrections.

    1.   Backing out of the garage, the trash can was in the way.
    2.   You should bathe the baby before taking a nap.
    3.   Smelling strongly of garlic, the sauce was ready.
    4.   Holding out her hand, the child took the gold coin.
    5.   Placing your ear to the seashell, the ocean can be heard.

F.   Is the underlined an appositive phrase **(AP)** or an adjective clause **(AC)**?

    1.   A man <u>who is known as Ike</u> lives next door.
    2.   My coat, <u>which has a blue collar and cuffs</u>, is in the cloak room.
    3.   Mrs. Clark, <u>recently named head librarian</u>, received her MLS at Berkeley.
    4.   Her father was sad <u>that Clementine had drowned</u> in the foaming brine.
    5.   Timing in comedy, <u>deciding where a laugh should be</u>, is not easy.

Answers

Clauses

Page 7
A. **D**ependent or **I**ndependent?

1. D
2. I
3. I
4. D
5. D

B. Dependent **C**lause or **P**hrase?

1. P
2. C
3. C
4. P
5. C
6. C

C. Underline dependent clauses.

1. <u>When my dog barks</u>, I jump.
2. I returned the sweater <u>that I had borrowed</u>.
3. Bob came, <u>as I had asked</u>, to the school.
4. <u>After you've watered the garden</u>, wash the windows.
5. Come over to my house <u>if you're not busy tonight</u>.

D. Underline the dependent clause and circle the word it modifies.

1. I like the ⟨dress⟩ <u>that has blue polka dots</u>.
2. My face ⟨turned⟩ red <u>when I tripped and fell</u>.
3. We ⟨moved⟩ twice <u>while Vanessa was still a baby</u>.
4. The cat will be ⟨mad⟩ <u>if you leave it out all night</u>.
5. The ⟨press,⟩ <u>before they could enter</u>, had to show identification.

E. Adv, Adj, or N?

1. N
2. Adv
3. Adj
4. N
5. Adv
6. Adj

Verbals and Phrases

Page 8
A. Verbal: Gerund, Participle, or Infinitive?

1. Part
2. Ger
3. Inf
4. Part
5. Ger

B. Phrase: Gerund, Participle, Infinitive, Prepositional, or Appositive?

1. Ger
2. Prep
3. Ger
4. App
5. Prep
6. Part
7. Ger
8. Inf
9. Part
10. Inf

C. Appositive or Participial Phrase?

1. Part
2. App
3. App
4. Part
5. App

D. Appositive phrases or Adjective clauses?

1. AP
2. AC
3. AP
4. AC
5. AP
6. AC

CLAUSES

Exercise A.

1. I love dogs. (I)
2. If I want a car. (D)
3. Barbara is a cheerleader. (I)
4. When I'm sixteen. (D)
5. If I go away to college. (D)
6. He would be king. (I)
7. The eagle soared. (I)
8. There were three bears. (I)
9. How the boy looked. (D)
10. Ever since the puppy licked my face. (D)

Exercise B.

1. **I**
2. **D**
3. **D**
4. **I**
5. **I**
6. **D**
7. **D**
8. **D**
9. **I**
10. **I**
11. **D**
12. **I**

Exercise C.

1. I'll return <u>after I run these errands</u>.
2. I have loved swimming <u>since I was three years old</u>.
3. <u>After I graduate</u>, I want to go to foreign lands.
4. The murderer came to the old mill <u>as Sherlock Holmes had expected</u>.
5. <u>Whatever the circumstances are</u>, Elena will understand.
6. <u>If I hurry through dinner</u>, I'll get an upset stomach.
7. The coat <u>that was by the door</u> is gone.
8. Shops close down around here <u>whenever it snows</u>.
9. She is a person <u>whom I have always admired</u>.
10. <u>When you get here</u>, I'll be ready to go.

Adverb Clauses

Exercise A. (Possible answers)

1. *Since* I take the bus every day
2. *After* Jenny is eighteen
3. *If* Donald had a motorcycle
4. *Until* June went away to college
5. *As long as* George has a degree in medicine
6. *Since* farmers expect drought this year
7. *As far as* I am concerned
8. *Before* Martha traveled in Japan
9. *Although* the bus was late
10. *Because* tomorrow is Friday
11. *While* roses are red
12. *When* JFK was President

Exercise B.

1. <u>If you'll go with us to the hills</u>, I'll prepare a picnic.
2. We had never been apart <u>until she went away to college</u>.
3. Sherman, <u>after he joined the Army</u>, went to Alabama for training.
4. <u>Since the water table dropped last spring</u>, they needed to ration water.
5. <u>Unless you've anything further to add</u>, I suggest we adjourn this meeting.
6. <u>Although Jerry has traveled throughout the U.S.,</u> he's never been to a foreign country.
7. I got to school on time <u>even though the bus was late</u>.
8. <u>While Joe helps kids with reading problems,</u> Jane teaches the hearing impaired.
9. Susan says she'll go <u>wherever Martin goes.</u>
10. Students were idealistic <u>when my mother was in college.</u>

Exercise C.

1. He is (confident) <u>before he takes tests</u>. **Adj**
2. Jenny (attends) college this fall <u>even though she is only sixteen</u>. **V**
3. Sue feels (better) <u>although she still has a cough</u>. **Adj**
4. Dad (works) two jobs <u>so that I can go to college</u>. **V**
5. Singing well didn't come (easily) <u>until I learned to relax</u>. **Adv**
6. <u>Since I didn't study</u>, I (flunked) the math exam. **V**

7. I (bought) a present for Harold because he fixed my tire last night. **V**
8. I am (safe) when you hold me. **Adj**
9. If I had known you were coming, I'd have (baked) a cake. **V**
10. He (eyed) my cone longingly while I took my first lick. **V**
11. You've never (seen) a sunset until you've been to Hawaii. **V**
12. Giselle is (happy) as long as she gets her way. **Adj**

Page 13 & 14
Exercise D. Answers will vary.

Exercise E.

1. I read the Wall Street Journal although it is too sophisticated for me. **concession**
2. Ever since I was a child, I've wanted to ride a horse. **time**
3. Jon is going to Stanford University because his dad went there.   **cause**
4. Unless the weather gets better, we'll all have to stay home. **condition**
5. Time will tell if I will reach my goals. **condition**
6. When you get to the party, call me. **time**
7. You are smarter than you think. **comparison**
8. As far as I can tell, it fits perfectly. **condition**
9. Though I've been to Disneyland often, I never tire of going there.   **concession**
10. You are not leaving until I know where you are going. **time**
11. I must live in France so that my French pronunciation will improve.   **purpose**
12. You look as if you have seen a ghost. **manner**

Adjective Clauses
Page 15
Exercise A.

1. The police found the dog *which Donald had lost.*
2. Little Jack Horner is the boy *whose Christmas pie was filled with plums.*
4. The place *where the swallows return every year* is Capistrano.
5. These books belong to Betty, *whose pencils I also borrowed.*
6. Maria, *whom I trust implicitly*, went to the bank for me.
7. Dr. Jonas Salk, *who discovered the oral polio vaccine*, continued research all his life.
8. Spring is the season *which I love the most.*

9. The lesson *that I've come to learn* is always tell the truth.
10. I love the ending *when Scarlett says, "Tomorrow is another day."*

Page 16
Exercise B.

1. The (doll) that I want is porcelain.
2. A (person) who speaks Russian will translate.
3. Could you get those (boxes) which I left in the corner?
4. (Madrid), which was hot, was a beautiful city.
5. The (scene) where Anna trips over Donald's foot is hilarious.
6. We appreciate the (donations) which we sorely need.
7. My (grandmother) whose birthday is next month, will be 98 years old.
8. The (dances) that are held on Fridays are sponsored by the Lions' Club.
9. Some (clauses), when they modify a noun or pronoun, are adjective clauses.
10. I put the broom in the (corner) where the chair is.

Page 17
Exercise C.

1. I like movies that are suspenseful. **R**
2. Ernest Hemingway is the only American author who always interests me. **R**
3. There is the dog that won first prize at the kennel show. **R**
4. She used the hose, which was 50 feet long, to water the garden. **N**
5. Your grandfather, who lived from 1898 to 1969, worked as an architect. **N**
6. Shoppers who wish to save money should buy here. **R**
7. Eugene Skinner, for whom the city of Eugene is named, was an early Oregon pioneer. **N**
8. Rugby, which is similar to football, is played worldwide. **N**
9. I decided to attend Mom's *Alma Mater*, which is Radcliff College. **N**
10. The ride to the airport, which usually takes fifteen minutes, took an hour. **N**

Exercise D.

1. Mary, who will be married Saturday, is my best friend.
2. Notice the part that I've set off with commas.
3. Lonnie, who is older than I, started college last year.
4. I'll have the spaghetti that we didn't eat last night.

5. You are someone <u>whom I don't understand</u>.
6. The car <u>that needs repair</u> is in the garage.
7. There was something wrong with the car <u>that we borrowed</u>.
8. All travelers <u>who arrive late</u> will miss their plane.
9. Emily, <u>who is my neighbor</u>, is on vacation.
10. This computer, <u>which is in use</u>, will be available after 3 o'clock.

Page 18 & 19
Exercise E.

1. When you say *that* man, of **whom** do you speak?
2. Mitzi, **who** is a star athlete, sprained her ankle.
3. The candidate for **whom** I campaigned was untruthful.
4. For **whom** does the bell toll?
5. Jack visited Ted, **who** graduated last year.
6. So you're the big lunk **who** sent the flowers. Thanks!

Exercise F.

1. The color **which (that)** I like best is chartreuse.
2. The puppy **that** I wanted to take home is gone.
3. Bob likes bungee jumping, **which** is a dangerous sport.
4. The Corvette, **which** belongs to Jon, is red.
5. It's time **that** I return home.
6. The food and clothes **that (which)** we collected will go to Bangladesh.

Exercise G. Suggested answers

1. It's time, **when the little hand is on the twelve**, to return home.
2. The person **who got me the job** is my cousin.
3. Madeleine won the gold medal **that I wanted**.
4. Madeleine, **whose father is a senator,** won the gold medal.
5. *Casablanca*, **which I've seen 12 times,** is a classic.
6. Peter, **when I need him most,** is always there.
7. I'd love to go to Brazil **where I can study its ancient culture.**
8. This is the country **that I'd love to visit**.
9. I plan to meet some movie stars **who have worked in Westerns**.
10. Marie hasn't met Mr. Bernard **whose work she greatly admires.**
11. My grandfather, **of whom I know little**, was an Olympic skier during the 1930s.
12. In Arizona, **where I used to live**, the desert wildflowers are beautiful.

Noun Clauses

Page 20
Exercise A.

1. I don't know <u>what happened</u>. **DO**
2. Good grades depend upon <u>how well you study</u> **OP**
3. The deciding factor is <u>whether or not your parents approve</u>. **PN**
4. Susan knew <u>that Tom would be there</u>. **DO**
5. <u>Whom do you trust</u> is the question. **S**
6. No one knows <u>where Donna lived</u>. **DO**
7. <u>Why he's being difficult</u> is anyone's guess. **S**
8. A concern of mine is <u>why you park in handicapped zones</u>. **PN**
9. Are you careful about <u>what you say to strangers</u>? **OP**
10. Mother understood <u>that I forgot to call</u>. **DO**

Page 21
Exercise B.

1. I will give it to *<u>whomever you designate</u>*. **OP**
2. *<u>What Mrs. Jamison said</u>* was hard for me to understand. **S**
3. To find warmer weather is *<u>why the birds fly South in winter</u>*. **PN**
4. Does Mother know *<u>where we are going tonight</u>*? **DO**
5. I want to know *<u>if you're okay</u>*. **DO**
6. *<u>Where the boys are</u>* is where the girls are. **S**
7. Leave a message with *<u>whoever answers the phone.</u>* **OP**
8. *<u>That I can hit a home run</u>* is a long shot. **S**
9. *<u>When the rivers run dry</u>* is a long time. **S**
10. I'll tell you *<u>whatever you want to know</u>*. **DO**

Page 22
Exercise C.

1. <u>Whoever needs a ride</u> is welcome to come with us. **N**
2. This is the (list) <u>which has the test scores</u>. **Adj**
3. I'm going to the (show) <u>that is at four o'clock</u>. **Adj**
4. <u>What I do with my life</u> is my business. **N**
5. I guess <u>that I'm the only (one)</u> <u>who voted this year</u>. **N,Adj**
6. <u>That I'm not responsible enough to drive</u> is not true. **N**
7. You mean the (one) <u>that is on the top shelf</u>? **Adj**
8. <u>Whatever John says</u> is all right by me. **N**
9. Don't take the (umbrella) <u>that has the red handle</u>. **Adj**
10. <u>How well I do</u> depends on <u>how hard I study</u>. **N, N**

VERBALS

Page 23

Pretest A.

1. Part
2. Ger
3. Inf
4. Part
5. Part
6. Inf
7. Ger
8. Inf

Pretest B.

1. N
2. Adj
3. Adv
4. N
5. N
6. Adj

Predicate Nominative or Progressive Tense

Page 25 & 26

Exercise A.

1. A good <u>exercise</u> is <u>swimming</u>.
2. My favorite winter <u>sport</u> is <u>skiing</u>.
3. Some childish <u>tactics</u> are <u>pouting</u> and <u>whining</u>.
4. A spring <u>pastime</u> in Japan is <u>writing</u> Haiku.
5. One sure <u>way</u> to get wrinkles is <u>smoking</u> cigarettes.

Exercise B.

1. Exercising is the way to become fit.
2. Believing is seeing.
3. A blessing is your great fortune.
4. Farming is one of the hardest jobs.
5. Failing civics is my worst nightmare.

Exercise C.

1. PV
2. PV
3. PN
4. PV
5. PN
6. PN
7. PV
8. PN
9. PV
10. PN

Gerund

Page 26

Exercise A. Subject

1. to swim
2. to jog
3. to dance
4. to shop
5. to hold
6. to time
7. to teach
8. to date
9. to eat
10. to dive

Exercise B. Predicate Nominative

1. John's (goal) was <u>winning</u>.
2. A dying American (art) is <u>quilting</u>.
3. Sarah's afternoon (ritual) was <u>swimming</u> and <u>sunning</u>.
4. Jody's (alibi) had been <u>sleeping</u>.
5. (Part) of growing up is <u>learning</u> to compromise.
6. The harshest (chore) for hands in the old days was <u>washing</u>.
7. A good (way) to improve your penmanship is <u>rewriting</u>.
8. The best (part) of cooking is <u>eating</u>.
9. Alexandra's (ambition) had always been <u>acting</u>.
10. An interesting (hobby) is stamp <u>collecting</u>.

Page 27

Exercise C. Direct Object.

1. He teaches <u>writing</u>.
2. Mary likes ice <u>skating</u>.
3. The children loved <u>watching</u> the game.
4. Bobby handled the grocery <u>shopping</u>.
5. Evelyn learned <u>shooting</u> from her father.
6. I like wind <u>surfing</u>.
7. Mother made the turkey <u>stuffing</u>.
8. Most kids like <u>studying</u> while the radio is on.
9. The juggler practiced <u>balancing</u> with one hand.
10. Stop <u>singing</u> so loud!

Exercise D. Object of Preposition

1. This book is (about) <u>hunting</u>.
2. The girls came (for) the <u>dancing</u>; the boys came for the food.
3. The lecture was (about) <u>drinking</u> and drugs.
4. (Before) <u>leaving</u>, please sign the roster.
5. He started to answer (without) <u>thinking</u>.

6. He won the trophy (by) working hard.
7. I was leaning (toward) writing the book myself.
8. The best (of) the singing was yet to come.
9. (By) telling about my trip, I was able to encourage others to travel.
10. When it comes (to) winning, Johnnie is the best.

Exercise E. Appositives

1. The water sport, underline{swimming}, is also good exercise.
2. Dad rarely finds time for his greatest pleasure, underline{fishing}.
3. One art in Japan, underline{drumming}, is called Taiko.
4. This spot will serve our purpose, underline{camping} and underline{hiking}.
5. Your destructive behavior, underline{fighting}, is more than I can stand.
6. She had an annoying habit, underline{interrupting}.
7. This task, underline{fencing}, is arduous for the rancher.
8. There's only one word for ocean waves, underline{calming}.
9. This task, underline{collating}, is a tedious part of mailing brochures.
10. The IRS has a challenging job, tax underline{collecting}.

Page 28
Exercise F. Suggested answers.

1. Mary likes underline{shopping}. **DO**
2. We don't allow hanging around, underline{loitering}, at this school. **App**
3. underline{Calling} should get results faster. **S**
4. Moving on your belly is underline{crawling}. **PN**
5. I've learned a lot about underline{saving}. **OP**
6. The room needs a Renoir underline{painting}. **DO**
7. underline{Closing} the door will keep out the draft. **S**
8. Long-range goals, underline{planning}, are important. **App**
9. Put the potatoes next to the underline{dressing}. **OP**
10. An important part of mowing is underline{edging}. **PN**

Participle

Page 29
Exercise A. Verb roots

1. **to swim**
2. **to hurt**
3. **to lose**
4. **to speak**
5. **to forget**
6. **to cry**
7. **to mow**
8. **to smile**
9. **to stand**
10. **to sit**

Exercise B. Adjective

1. swimming
2. pickled
3. jumping
4. dried
5. shorn
6. boxing
7. hearing
8. buried
9. grown
10. Tested

Page 30
Exercise C. Participle or verb

1. **V**
   Part
2. **V**
   Part
3. **Part**
   V, V
4. **V**
   Part
5. **V**
   Part
6. **Part**
   V
7. **V**
   Part
8. **Part**
   V
9. **Part**
   V
10. **Part**
    V

Exercise D.

1. **Ger**
2. **Part, Part**
3. **Ger**
4. **Ger, PV**
5. **Ger, Part**
6. **Ger, Ger**
7. **PV, V, V**
8. **Ger, Ger**
9. **PV**
10. **Part**
11. **Part**
12. **Part**
13. **PV**
14. **V, V**
15. **Ger, Part**

Infinitive

Page 32
Exercise A. Noun

1. To get **S**
2. to believe **DO**
3. to listen **DO**
4. to ask **DO**
5. To cooperate **S**
6. to dance **DO**
7. **no infinitive**
8. to be **DO**
9. To teach **S**
10. to leave **DO**

Exercise B. Adjective

1. to read modifies **book**
2. to eat modifies **fudge**
3. to beat modifies **guy**
4. to do modifies **thing**
5. to shine modifies **time**
6. to keep modifies **secret**
7. to begin modifies **time**
8. to climb modifies **energy**

Exercise C. Adverb

1. to return modifies **happy** **Adj**
2. to find out modifies **stayed** **V**
3. to hear modifies **listened** **V**
4. to go modifies **ready** **Adj**
5. to pass modifies **enough** **Adv**
6. to see modifies **sad** **Adj**
7. to strengthen modifies **have been exercising** **V**
8. to walk modifies **too** **Adv**

Page 33
Exercise D. Infinitives

1. I want to be alone. **DO**
2. Bob hurried to finish his homework. **Adv**
3. Mother decided to take a ceramics class. **Adv**
4. To win feels great. **S**
5. Sally plans to attend. **DO**
6. She studied hard to earn her diploma. **Adv**
7. This crossword is hard to do. **Adv**
8. To complain was a mistake. **S**
9. Children need something to do all the time. **Adj**
10. Mary bought a special dress to wear. **Adj**
11. Are you trying to scare me? **Adv**
12. Your house is difficult to find at night. **Adv**

PHRASES

Page 35 & 36
Exercise A.

1. **single**
2. **phrase**
3. **phrase**
4. **single**
5. **single**
6. **single**
7. **single**
8. **single/single**
9. **phrase/single**
10. **phrase**

Exercise B.

1. **verbal** (participle), **prepositional**
2. **verbal** (participle), **prepositional**
3. **appositive, verbal** (infinitive)
4. **appositive**
5. **prepositional**
6. **prepositional**
7. **verbal** (participle), **prepositional**
8. **verbal** (infinitive)
9. **prepositional**, **appositive**
10. **verbal** (participle)

Gerund Phrases

Page 37 & 38
Exercise A.

1. Going along with the crowd **S**
2. Honing his tennis skill **S**
3. lying on your back **DO**
4. Identifying the gerund **S**
5. swimming in our pool **DO**
6. Falling off a bicycle **S**
7. standing up for yourself **DO**
8. Substituting sweetener for sugar **S**
9. filling in the blanks **DO**
10. Standing up for yourself **S**

Exercise B. Suggested answers.

1. **pitching** *a no hitter* **PN**
2. **Allowing** *you to drive* **S**
3. **collecting** *baseball cards* **DO**
4. **helping** *people in need.* **DO**
5. **working** *at the factory* **App**
6. *before* **eating** **OP**
7. **shielding** *their children from harm* **PN**
8. *The* **sentencing** *for the criminals* **S**
9. *After* **drinking** *alcohol* **OP**
10. **Studying** *for the exam* **S**
11. **restoring** *that old building* **PN**
12. **Learning** *to tie shoelaces* **S**

Exercise C. Suggested answers.

1. <u>Walking in the park</u> is peaceful. **S**
2. The best part of Joey's morning is <u>attending day care</u>. **PN**
3. I don't worry about <u>spending too much money</u>. **OP**
4. My uncle enjoys <u>living as a hermit</u>.   **DO**
5. My job, <u>working at the dime store</u>, is very rewarding. **App**
6. Sarah likes <u>feeding the animals</u>. **DO**
7. <u>Choosing the right person for the job</u> requires careful screening. **S**
8. The president's quest, <u>choosing the right person for the job</u>, has been completed. **App**
9. I need <u>complete understanding</u> **DO**
10. A good way to learn this book is <u>testing each other</u> on the exercises. **PN**

Page 39
Exercise D.

1. **PN** <u>pruning trees to remain small</u>
2. **PV**
3. **PV**
4. **PN** <u>fishing at the old river pond</u>
5. **PV**
6. **PV**
7. **PN** <u>relaxing in the tub</u>
8. **PN** <u>playing at the Hungry I</u>
9. **PV**
10. **PN** <u>soothing to the ear.</u>

Exercise E.

1. **OP**
2. **App**
3. **PN**
4. **S**
5. **DO**

6. **S**
7. **OP**
8. **App**
9. **DO**
10. **PN**

Page 40
Exercise F. Answers will vary. Good luck!

Participial Phrases

Page 41
Exercise A.

1. That noise (coming) from the engine of my car really worries me.
2. (Ruined) by the rain, the dress could never be worn again.
3. Now (roasted) to a golden brown, the turkey was ready to eat.
4. These words (coming) from your father require your attention.
5. Rock music records (collected) by my father are now classics.
6. My brother, (hunting) in the backwoods at thirteen, found a baby fox.
7. (Feeling) good, the three boys pitched in to buy ice cream cones.
8. The demented scientist (creeping) toward the heroine was played by Lon Chaney.
9. Extra caution must be taken by those students (driving) their cars.
10. Stealth bombs (launched) at night are very scary.

Page 42
Exercise B.

1. That (noise) coming from the engine of my car really worries me.
2. Ruined by the rain, the (dress) could never be worn again.
3. That tiny (kitten) sitting alone in the corner, is the one I want.
4. Clearly chirping away, the (canary) hadn't a care in the world.
5. Rock (music) collected by my father is now a classic.
6. My (brother) hunting in the backwoods at thirteen, found a baby fox.
7. Feeling good, the three (boys) pitched in to buy ice cream cones.
8. The demented (scientist) creeping toward the heroine was Lon Chaney.

9. Extra caution must be taken by those (students) driving their cars.
10. Stealth (bombs) launched at night are very scary.

Exercise C.

1. coming from the cemetery? **Prep**
2. Listening acutely **Adv**
3. mocking her brother **N Comp**
4. Carrying his daughter **N Comp**
5. running across the back lawn **Prep**
6. living in Arkansas as a youth **Prep, N Comp**
7. The old, starved buzzard **single Adj**
8. playing in the stream **Prep**
9. exquisitely carved. **Adv**
10. Launched nightly **Adv**

Exercise D.

1. the screeching of the brakes **Ger**
2. shaking violently **Part**
3. Wearing only a nightshirt **Part**
4. had been sleeping **PV**
5. the sharp barking **Ger**
6. streaked across the road **Part**
7. tired of telling the story **Part**
8. falling asleep quickly **Ger**
9. were sleeping peacefully **PV**
10. Holding his hand tightly **Part**

Page 43
Exercise E. Punctuating Phrases

1. *Assuming a relaxed attitude,* Bobby walked onto the stage.
2. Jill loved wool skirts and sweaters *woven in Ireland.* **none**
3. Marty, *completely absorbed in the book,* hadn't noticed me.
4. The cookies *baked by Joan's mother* are chocolate chip. **none**
5. Corinne, *afraid of getting wet,* waited inside the building.
6. She forgot her homework *lying on the kitchen table.* **none**
7. *Having fought the good fight,* the football team headed for the showers.
8. The scream *coming from the building* alarmed me. **none**
9. Tell those dogs *barking in the backyard* to stop.
10. *Assured of winning the gold,* Maria began to relax a little.

Page 44
Exercise F. Misplaced Modifiers

1. That noise **coming from my engine** really worries me.
2. That puppy **sitting alone in the corner** is the one I want.
3. My brother, **hunting in the woods,** found a baby fox.
4. My sister, **playing her violin,** is in another world.
5. The race car, **screeching out of control,** ran into the embankment.
6. My brother found a raccoon **caught in a trap.**
7. All week I had a cold **in the nose.**
8. He discovered his windbreaker **hanging on a hook in the closet.**
9. The prospector, **using his Geiger counter,** found uranium.
10. I hid the dress, **ruined by the rain,** so Mother wouldn't see.

Page 45
Exercise G. Dangling Participles (answers may vary)

1. Awakened suddenly, I felt the night seemed oddly silent.
2. Listening at the door, Mary heard an argument.
3. Wearing a new designer suit, he confidently entered the executive's office.
4. Approaching from the front entrance, I thought the theater was impressive.
5. Searching under the bed, I found the kitten peering out at me.
6. Driving through the Redwood Forest, we saw several deer.
7. As she focused the microscope, she could see bacteria.
8. Turning the wheel sharply, I lost control of the car and crashed into the railing.
9. I had to stand up to eat.
10. He developed a cold from sleeping in the rain.

Infinitive Phrases

Page 47
Exercise A. Noun

1. The toughest part of the test will be (to answer) the essay questions. **PN**
2. I want (to drive) to the show. **DO**

67

3. To know your own mind shows you're growing up. **S**
4. Mary refused to walk to school today. *DO*
5. I'm planning to attend the conference. *DO*
6. To bend the rules for you would indicate that I'm wishy-washy. **S**
7. The hardest lesson you'll ever learn is to show humility. **PN**
8. To set a good example for your brother is a heavy burden. **S**
9. I don't want to sit here alone. **DO**
10. Your job before you leave the house is to make your bed. **PN**

Exercise B.   Adjective

1. Judy's the one to watch in the swimming competition.
2. We get pork chops to eat tonight.
3. Judy has the right to speak out on these issues.
4. I had a chance to get a bargain.
5. The person to follow out the door is Judy.
6. We were the first to buy tickets to the concert.
7. The firemen were the only people to notice the gathering crowd.
8. Your trip to see the famous Wellington Gardens sounds fascinating.
9. The first person to finish in under two minutes will set a record.
10. I know it is a heavy burden to set a good example for your brother.

Exercise C.   Adverb.

1. I'm sorry to hear the news. **Adj**
2. Bill really stretched to catch the fly ball. **V**
3. We were too tired to continue the search. **Adv**
4. Mary tiptoed to keep from being heard. **V**
5. I was pleased to appear on television. **Adj**
6. She labored to discover the cause of the disease. **V**
7. Graham had studied enough to pass his test. **Adv**
8. Stan shopped to make himself happy. **V**
9. Emily seemed content to read for long hours. **Adj**
10. We all ran to see the fire. **V**

Page 48
Exercise D.

1. **Adv**
2. **Adj**
3. **S**
4. **Adv**
5. **PN**
6. **Adj**
7. **Adv**
8. **DO**
9. **Adj**
10. **S**
11. **DO**
12. **Adv**

Exercise E. Suggested answers.

1. **To drive a car** gives me a powerful feeling.
2. She read diligently **to select the best college.**
3. Do you want **to let the bird go free?**
4. It's your chance **to solve the problem**.
5. My job is **to collect insurance**.
6. He's bound **to benefit from the experience.**
7. **To choose a puppy** is an important decision.
8. She was the last person **to get to the game**.
9. Monica is hurrying **to grow up**.
10. His intent is **to get a good job.**

Prepositional Phrases

Page 49 & 50
Exercise A. Suggested answers.

1. at *the park*
2. beneath *the tree*
3. from *the mountains*
4. below *the tree line*
5. past *the fence*
6. next to *my briefcase*
7. on *a clear day*
8. behind *door number one*
9. toward *daybreak*
10. about *the homework*

Exercise B. (As adjectives) Suggested answers.

1. Earthquakes *near San Francisco* are especially dangerous.
2. My baby brother said he heard the reindeer *upon our roof.*
3. I'm driving to Monterey *to the Blues Festival.*
4. The snow *beneath my feet* was slushy.
5. The reeds *in the river* swayed.
6. I received a call *from my aunt.*
7. The wind *outside my door* blew in gusts.
8. The sun *toward the west now* has turned red.
9. The boy *with red hair* was mischievous.
10. The sun *over head* bleached the sky white.

Exercise C. (As adverbs) Suggested answers.

1. We saw an oppossum run *across our back yard*
2. She'll feel better *in a few hours.*
3. The books cost *about $3.00 each.*
4. He succeeded *by careful, hard work.*
5. The choice *between cake or pie* was difficult.
6. She tries to be nice *for visitors.*
7. We can meet *outside the library.*
8. The kitten hid *under the bed .*
9. Lots of people were coughing *during the performance.*
10. I'll sit *beside the bed* until you feel better.

Page 51
Exercise D.

1. The (senator) from Tennessee spoke. **Adj**
2. The senator from Tennessee (spoke) for 45 minutes. **Adv**
3. We (stayed) on her houseboat. **Adv**
4. We stayed on the (houseboat) on the Sacramento River. **Adj**
5. The (drive) to the general store was fun. **Adj**
6. (Driving) in the Model A to the general store was fun. **Adv**
7. Driving once again to the general (store) near Wedge Creek was fun. **Adj**
8. The (eagle) above me soared. **Adj**
9. Above me, the soaring eagle (was searching) for food. **Adv**
10. The eagle (soared) effortlessly above me. **Adv**

Exercise E.

1. We went (to) the party together. **Adv**
2. The trip (to) Yosemite Natinal Park was the highlight (of) my senior year. **Adj/Adj**
3. Bobby will drive me (to) your house (before) noon. **Adv/Adv**
4. Mary hopes to sing (with) the Metropolitan Opera Company someday. **Adv**
5. Mr. Graham told me to stand (between) the goal posts. **Adv**
6. Dancing (in) the moonlight is very romantic. **Adv**
7. My family has known Mr. and Mrs. Downs (for) many years. **Adv**
8. I'll be ready (in) a minute! **Adv**
9. I knew (in) a moment it must be St. Nick. **Adv**
10. Have you seen my jacket (with) the yellow buttons? **Adj**
11. I want to visit Paris (during) the springtime. **Adv**
12. The sand is cool (under) the boardwalk. **Adv**
13. The puppy (upon) the porch is mine. **Adj**
14. **none**
15. I'm just mad (about) Saffron. **Adv**

Appositive Phrases

Page 52 & 53
Exercise A.

1. (Spring) the season of renewal, is the best time to view cherry blossoms.
2. I often go to my aunt's (guesthouse) the cottage on Bridge Street, after school.
3. My dad plays the (clarinet) his favorite instrument.
4. I used to play (Old Maid,) an old-fashioned card game, as a child.
5. My golf (ball) a nubby green comet, hit a tree before dropping into the hole.
6. (Bonsai,) the Japanese art of growing miniature trees, instills awe within me.
7. Joe's Master's (thesis) a paper chronicling 14th Century Russia, was brilliant.
8. I was up at (1 a.m.,) the ghostly hour of the night.
9. Zane Grey's (books) vivid descriptions of the Southwest, are very exciting.
10. (The Grapes of Wrath) a book about the Dust-Bowl Era, was made into a movie.

Exercise B.

1. **AP**
2. **AC**
3. **AP**
4. **AC**
5. **AP**
6. **AC**
7. **AP**
8. **AC**
9. **AC**
10. **AP**

Exercise C. Fill in the blanks.

1. the Salk vaccine
2. *Mondo Kane*
3. best in show
4. that special stew Mother made last night
5. the symbol for *and*
6. the act of making life easier to understand
7. a much needed respite
8. a nervous giggle
9. the Queen and the Double
10. a popular children's book

Page 54
Exercise D.

1. <u>running the one-minute mile</u> **PP**
2. <u>searing hot metal</u> **AP**
3. <u>gagged and bound with tape</u> **PP**
4. <u>farmers from Iowa and Kansas</u> **AP**
5. <u>concernng the new health care plan</u> **PP**
6. <u>my party tomorrow night</u> **AP**

Exercise E. Suggested answers

1. We were aware of Mr. Chan's cigar, an acrid smell, three floors away.
2. Gary Cooper, the tall and handsome stranger, was a popular screen idol.
3. The puppy, a fluffy Samoyed, was curled into a small white ball.
4. Bells, wind-blown noisemakers, hung from the porch.
5. Alone at the light, the hot-rodder revved his engine impatiently.

Clauses

Page 55 & 56
A.   Adverb, adjective, or noun clauses

1. Leslie finally knows <u>why good grades are important to his future</u>. **N**
2. <u>Whichever team I choose</u> is sure to win. **N**
3. Africa, <u>which is a huge country</u>, has many different tribes. **Adj**
4. I'll be stationed in Somalia, <u>where the Peace Corps is needed so much</u>. **Adj**
5. He knew <u>where to find the body</u>. **N**
6. The party starts <u>when you arrive</u>. **Adv**
7. Is this the way <u>which is best</u>? **Adj**
8. Call me from <u>wherever you are</u>. **N**
9. Watson came <u>after Sherlock had called</u>. **Adv**
10. He came to make new friends <u>who enjoyed playing chess</u>. **Adj**

B.   Noun clauses as the subject, direct object, predicate nominative, or object of preposition.

1. We'll take <u>whichever route is quicker</u>. **DO**
2. <u>Whoever makes a ruckus</u> goes directly home. **S**
3. I'm not sure about <u>where I'll be staying in France</u>. **OP**
4. Five dollars is <u>how much money you'll need</u>. **PN**
5. Martin is taking <u>whoever says "yes" first</u> to the prom. **DO**

C.   Adverb clause modifying a verb, an adjective, or an adverb.

1. Jennie (jumped) <u>after I yelled "boo!"</u> **V**
2. David was (cautious) <u>while he drove his dad's car</u>. **Adj**
3. This pie tastes (good) <u>even though I don't usually eat rhubarb</u>. **Adj**
4. I feel (better) <u>than I did a week ago.</u> **Adj**
5. Fido (eyed) the mailman warily <u>until he was out of sight</u>. **V**
6. We (can ride) together <u>unless you'd prefer to drive your own car</u>. **V**

D. Adjective clause or noun clause.

1. The duckling that had been ugly became a beautiful swan. **Adj**
2. The butterfly exemplifies that which is elusive in life. **Adj**
3. Dorothy asked about which road leads to the Emerald City. **N**
4. Who had asked the question in the first place had been long forgotten. **N**
5. That singer who sang the aria also likes to sing jazz. **Adj**

Final Assessment Test

Verbals and Phrases

Page 56 & 57
A. Underline verbals.

1. My father has a sprained back. **Part**
2. The worst part of having a cold is the coughing. **Ger/Ger**
3. Listening is part of learning. **Ger/Ger**
4. I was taught to control my anger in public. **Inf**
5. Have you seen the soldering iron? **Part**
6. Placing the cool towel on my brow helped to soothe my fever. **Ger/Inf**
7. The solemn-faced boy stood bravely. **None**
8. Rolfing is a technique for improving one's posture. **Ger/Ger**
9. "Sufferin' succotash!" cried Sylvester, the cat. **Part**
10. It is time to change for dinner. **Inf**

B. Underline gerund, participle, infinitive, prepositional, or appositive phrases.

1. Pressing our ears against the ground, we could hear the train coming. **Ger/Prep**
2. The dog, scratching his ear, groaned with ecstasy. **Part/Prep**
3. You can be sure to count on me. **Inf/Prep**
4. Are you going to the opera tomorrow night? **Prep**
5. It's only a game, a silly prank, for your benefit. **App/Prep**
6. Why, I do believe that girl is seething with envy! **Prep**
7. The Munchkins, pointing the way to Oz, wore bright colors that day. **Part/Prep**
8. To simplify matters even further, I suggest that we all go together. **Inf**

9. I've seen *Wizard of Oz*, a whimsical musical, seventeen times. **App**
10. The lawyer specializing in accident claims has an office in this building. **Part/Prep**

C. Punctuate the following with commas where necessary.

1. None
2. Sometimes, when I'm lonely, I think of you.
3. If you are in the neighborhood, drop by.
4. None
5. None

D. Misplaced modifying phrases. Suggested changes.

1. The books, faded from age, were given away.
2. I'll drop by to pick up my sister when it's convenient for you.
3. He ran after the ball with the glove held high.
4. Donna, as a working mother, still manages to keep her home immaculate.
5. The greasy spoon, which you forgot to wash, is on the counter.

E. Dangling participial phrases. Suggested changes.

1. The trash can was in the way as I was backing out of the garage.
2. You should bathe the baby before putting him down for a nap.
3. OK
4. OK
5. By placing your ear to the seashell, you can hear the ocean.

F. Appositive phrase **(AP)** or adjective clause **(AC)**.

1. **AC**
2. **AC**
3. **AP**
4. **AC**
5. **AP**

Math Series

The Straight Forward Math Series

is systematic, first diagnosing skill levels, then *practice*, periodic *review*, and *testing*.

Blackline

GP-006 Addition
GP-012 Subtraction
GP-007 Multiplication
GP-013 Division
GP-039 Fractions
GP-083 Word Problems, Book 1

The Advanced Straight Forward Math Series

is a higher level system to diagnose, practice, review, and test skills.

Blackline

GP-015 Advanced Addition
GP-016 Advanced Subtraction
GP-017 Advanced Multiplication
GP-018 Advanced Division
GP-020 Advanced Decimals
GP-021 Advanced Fractions
GP-044 Mastery Tests
GP-028 Pre-Algebra, Book 1
GP-029 Pre-Algebra, Book 2
GP-030 Pre-Geometry, Book 1
GP-031 Pre-Geometry, Book 2

Large Editions

Blackline

GP-037 Algebra, Book 1
GP-038 Algebra, Book 2
GP-045 Trigonometry
GP-054 Geometry
GP-053 Pre-Calculus
GP-064 Calculus AB, Vol. 1
GP-067 Calculus AB, Vol. 2

Applied Math Series

The Applied Math Series

is designed for those who wonder how various mathematic disciplines can be used to solve everyday problems.

GP-063 Applying Algebra
GP-070 Metrics at Work
GP-080 Solving Word Problems
GP-084 Basic Equations

English Series

The Straight Forward English S

is designed to measure, teach, review, and master specified English skills: capitalization and punctuat nouns and pronouns; verbs; adjectives and adverb: prepositions, conjunctions and interjections; senter clauses and phrases, and mechanics.

Each workbook is a simple, straightforward approa learning English skills. Skills are keyed to major sct textbook adoptions.

Pages are reproducible.

GP-032	Capitalization and Punctuation
GP-033	Nouns and Pronouns
GP-034	Verbs
GP-035	Adjectives and Adverbs
GP-041	Sentences
GP-043	Prepositions, conjunctions, & Interjections

Advanced Series

Large editions

GP-055	Clauses & Phrases
GP-056	Mechanics
GP-075	Grammar & Diagramming Sentences

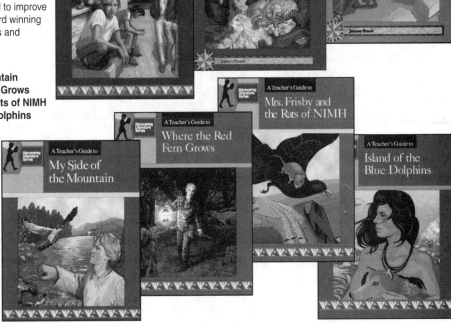

Discovering Literature Series

The Discovering Literature Series

is designed to develop an appreciation for literature and to improve reading skills. Each guide in the series features an award winning novel and explores a wide range of critical reading skills and literature elements.

GP-076	A Teaching Guide to My Side of the Mountain
GP-077	A Teaching Guide to Where the Red Fern Grows
GP-078	A Teaching Guide to Mrs. Frisby & the Rats of NIMH
GP-079	A Teaching Guide to Island of the Blue Dolphins
GP-093	A Teaching Guide to the Outsiders
GP-094	A Teaching Guide to Roll of Thunder

Challenging Level

GP-090	The Hobbit: A Teaching Guide
GP-091	Redwall: A Teaching Guide
GP-092	The Odyssey: A Teaching Guide
GP-097	The Giver: A Teaching Guide